The Complete Diabetic Diet Cookbook for 2023

1800 Mouth-watering Low-sugar Recipes to Control Blood Sugar, Slow Down Ageing and Achieve a Sustainable Healthy Diet with 28-Day Meal Plans

Angela D. Fouts

All Rights Reserved.

The content contained within this book may not be reproduced, duplicated, or transmitted without direct written permission from the author or the publisher. Under no circumstances will any blame or legal responsibility be held against the publisher, or author, for any damages, reparation, or monetary loss due to the information contained within this book, either directly or indirectly.

Legal Notice: This book is copyright protected. It is only for personal use. You cannot amend, distribute, sell, use, quote or paraphrase any part, or the content within this book, without the consent of the author or publisher.

Disclaimer Notice:

Please note the information contained within this document is for educational and entertainment purposes only. All effort has been executed to present accurate, up to date, reliable, complete information. No warranties of any kind are declared or implied. Readers acknowledge that the author is not engaged in the rendering of legal, financial, medical, or professional advice. The content within this book has been derived from various sources. Please consult a licensed professional before attempting any techniques outlined in this book. By reading this document, the reader agrees that under no circumstances is the author responsible for any losses, direct or indirect, that are incurred as a result of the use of the information contained within this document, including, but not limited to, errors, omissions, or inaccuracies.

CONTENTS

Introduction 7
What exactly is diabetes? 8
Dietary requirements for diabetes? 8
What are the health benefits of following a diabetes diet? 9

Breakfast Recipes 10
Popcorn With Olive Oil 10
Southwest Breakfast Pockets 10
Avocado And Bean Toast 11
Sausage-egg Burritos 11
Toasted Corn Salsa 12
Sweet Onion Frittata With Ham 12
Breakfast Tacos 13
Crunchy French Toast 13
Raspberry Peach Puff Pancake 14
Marinated Artichokes 14
Cheesy Baked Grits 15
Kale Chips 15
Crispy Polenta Squares With Olives And Sun-dried Tomatoes 16
Egg & Hash Brown Breakfast Cups 16

Appetizers And Snacks Recipes 17
Zesty Lemony Shrimp 17
Avocado Endive Boats 17
Dilled Chex Toss 18
Bleu Cheese'd Pears 18
Chicken, Mango & Blue Cheese Tortillas 18
Raisin & Hummus Pita Wedges 19
Roasted Red Pepper Tapenade 19
Crostini With Kalamata Tomato 19
Blueberry Salsa 20
Garden-fresh Wraps 20
Baked Pot Stickers With Dipping Sauce 21
Minutesi Feta Pizzas 21
Meatballs In Cherry Sauce 22
Lime'd Blueberries 22

Poultry Recipes 23
Southwest-style Shepherd's Pie 23
Turkey-thyme Stuffed Peppers 23
Sausage Orecchiette Pasta 24
Country Roast Chicken With Lemony Au Jus 24
Avocado And Green Chili Chicken 25
Braised Chicken Breasts With Chickpeas And Chermoula 25
Baked Chicken Chalupas 26
Pan-seared Chicken Breasts With Leek And White Wine Pan Sauce 26
Sausage And Farro Mushrooms 27
Quick & Easy Turkey Sloppy Joes 27

Spring Chicken & Pea Salad 28
Bacon & Swiss Chicken Sandwiches 28
Lemon Chicken With Orzo 29
Turkey Shepherd's Pie 30

Fish & Seafood Recipes 31

Shrimp-slaw Pitas 31
Garlic-herb Salmon Sliders 31
Poached Snapper With Sherry-tomato Vinaigrette 32
Shrimp And Sausage Rice 32
Lemon-pepper Tilapia With Mushrooms 33
Tomato-poached Halibut 33
Salmon Cakes With Lemon-herb Sauce 34
Black Rice Bowls With Salmon 34
Shrimp Piccata 35
Pan-seared Sesame-crusted Tuna Steaks 35
Two-sauce Cajun Fish 36
Creamy Dill Sauce 36
Cod In Coconut Broth With Lemon Grass And Ginger 37
Fantastic Fish Tacos 37

Vegetables, Fruit And Side Dishes Recipes 38

Roasted Beans And Green Onions 38
Orzo With Peppers & Spinach 38
Sautéed Spinach With Yogurt And Dukkah 39
Basil Grilled Corn On The Cob 39
Broiled Eggplant With Basil 39
Crunchy Pear And Cilantro Relish 40
Roasted Root Vegetables With Lemon-caper Sauce 40
Sautéed Swiss Chard With Garlic 40
Balsamic Zucchini Saute 41
Pesto Pasta & Potatoes 41
Tomato-onion Green Beans 41
Marinated Eggplant With Capers And Mint 42
Sautéed Green Beans With Garlic And Herbs 42
Saucy Eggplant And Capers 42

Vegetarian Recipes 43

Chickpea Cakes With Cucumber-yogurt Sauce 43
Stewed Chickpeas With Eggplant And Tomatoes 44
Mexican-style Spaghetti Squash Casserole 44
Sweet Potato, Poblano, And Black Bean Tacos 45
Light Parmesan Pasta 45
Stuffed Eggplant With Bulgur 46
Curried Tempeh With Cauliflower And Peas 47
Cheesy Spinach-stuffed Shells 47
Vegan Black Bean Burgers 48
Eggplant Involtini 49
Sautéed Spinach With Chickpeas And Garlicky Yogurt 49
Ricotta-stuffed Portobello Mushrooms 50
"refried" Bean And Rice Casserole 50
Tunisian-style Grilled Vegetables With Couscous And Eggs 51

Salads Recipes 52
Roasted Winter Squash Salad With Za'atar And Parsley 52
Broccoli & Apple Salad 52
Spicy Chipotle Chicken Salad With Corn 53
Tangy Sweet Carrot Pepper Salad 53
Classic Wedge Salad 54
Garden Bounty Potato Salad 54
Shrimp Salad With Avocado And Grapefruit 55
Michigan Cherry Salad 55
Toasted Pecan And Apple Salad 56
Warm Cabbage Salad With Chicken 56
Walnut Vinaigrette 57
Arugula Salad With Fennel And Shaved Parmesan 57
Brussels Sprout Salad With Pecorino And Pine Nuts 58
Warm Spinach Salad With Apple, Blue Cheese, And Pecans 58

Meat Recipes 59
Peppered Beef Tenderloin 59
Cajun Beef & Rice 59
Spinach Steak Pinwheels 60
Smoky Sirloin 60
Chili Sloppy Joes 61
Cabbage Roll Skillet 61
One-pot Beef & Pepper Stew 62
Cumin'd Beef Patties And Santa Fe Sour Cream 62
Steak Tacos With Jícama Slaw 63
Sweet Jerk Pork 63
Quick Hawaiian Pizza 64
Braised Pork Stew 64
Sunday Pork Roast 65
Spicy Chili'd Sirloin Steak 65

Special Treats Recipes 66
Frozen Chocolate Monkey Treats 66
Lemon Cupcakes With Strawberry Frosting 66
Chocolate-dipped Strawberry Meringue Roses 67
Turkish Stuffed Apricots With Rose Water And Pistachios 67
Mini Chocolate Cupcakes With Creamy Chocolate Frosting 68
Dark Chocolate–avocado Pudding 68
Cream Cheese Swirl Brownies 69
Grilled Angel Food Cake With Strawberries 69
No-fuss Banana Ice Cream 69
Citrus Gingerbread Cookies 70
Roasted Pears With Cider Sauce 70
Saucy Spiced Pears 71
Individual Summer Berry Gratins 71
Fig Bars 72

Slow Cooker Favorites Recipes 73
Hearty Turkey Soup With Swiss Chard 73
Braised Fennel With Orange-tarragon Dressing 73
Catalan Beef Stew 74

Thai-style Pork 74
Chicken Thighs With Black-eyed Pea Ragout 75
Slow Cooker Split Pea Soup 75
Slow Cooker Mushroom Chicken & Peas 76
Pork Loin With Fennel, Oranges, And Olives 76
Mediterranean Pot Roast Dinner 77
Slow Cooker Beef Tostadas 77
Spiced Carrots & Butternut Squash 78
No-fuss Quinoa With Lemon 78
Chicken With Warm Potato And Radish Salad 79
Parsley Smashed Potatoes 79

Potatoes, Pasta, And Whole Grains Recipes 80
Penne With Butternut Squash And Sage 80
Brown Rice With Tomatoes And Chickpeas 81
Tabbouleh 81
Lentils With Spinach And Garlic Chips 82
Easy Greek-style Chickpea Salad 82
Country Stuffed Summer Squash 83
Turkey And Cheese Lasagna 83
Paprika Roasted Potatoes 84
Pasta Alla Norma With Olives And Capers 84
Cuban Black Beans 85
Black-eyed Peas With Walnuts And Pomegranate 85
Pasta'd Mushrooms 86
Bulgur Salad With Carrots And Almonds 86
Farro Salad With Asparagus, Snap Peas, And Tomatoes 87

Soups, Stews, And Chilis Recipes 88
Autumn Bisque 88
Chickpea And Kale Soup 88
Vegetarian Chili 89
Very Veggie Soup 89
Hearty Ten Vegetable Stew 90
Sweet Corn And Peppers Soup 90
Smoky Tomato Pepper Soup 91
Chicken Tortilla Soup With Greens 91
Butternut Squash And White Bean Soup With Sage Pesto 92
Black Bean-tomato Chili 92
Pumpkin Turkey Chili 93
Tomato-orange Soup 93
New England Fish Stew 94
Mushroom And Wheat Berry Soup 94

28 day meal plan 95

INDEX 97

Introduction

Welcome to the culinary journey that is "The Complete Diabetic Diet Cookbook for 2023". I'm Angela D. Fouts, your guide and fellow traveler on this path to better health. For those who are meeting me for the first time, let me tell you a little about myself. I'm a certified dietitian, cookbook author, and I have a deeply personal relationship with diabetes - a condition that has touched my family and motivated me to dedicate my life to helping others manage it.

This collection of recipes is designed not only to meet the nutritional needs of those managing diabetes, but also to please the palate of anyone who loves good food. From hearty breakfasts to comforting main dishes, from light bites to satisfying desserts, each dish was crafted with health, balance, and flavor in mind. This book is more than just a collection of recipes. It's a tool, a guide, and a friend to help you navigate the complex journey of managing diabetes through food. I believe that eating should be a joy, not a chore, and certainly not something to fear, even for those with dietary restrictions.

The goal of this cookbook is not just about managing your glucose levels, it's also about embracing a healthier lifestyle that enhances your overall wellbeing. This journey is about discovering that a diet tailored for diabetes can also be delicious, diverse, and satisfying.

As you explore the pages and recipes of this book, I hope it inspires you in your kitchen and uplifts your spirits, proving that a diabetes-friendly diet can be a gateway to a world of culinary delight. Here's to creating meals that fuel our bodies and nourish our souls!

So, let's begin this journey together, armed with an open mind, a hungry stomach, and the power to take control of our health.

What exactly is diabetes?

Diabetes is a chronic disease that affects how your body turns food into energy. It is characterized by high levels of sugar (glucose) in the blood. This condition is primarily due to either the body's inability to produce insulin or its inability to use insulin effectively, or sometimes both.

Most of the food you eat is broken down into glucose (sugar) and released into your bloodstream. When your blood sugar goes up, it signals your pancreas to release insulin. Insulin is a hormone that acts like a key, allowing the glucose to enter your cells to be used as energy.

There are a few different types of diabetes:

- **Type 1 Diabetes:** This is an autoimmune disease where the body's immune system attacks and destroys the insulin-producing cells in the pancreas. It's usually diagnosed in children and young adults, but it can occur at any age. People with type 1 diabetes need to take insulin every day to stay alive.

- **Type 2 Diabetes:** This is a metabolic disorder that results from the body becoming resistant to insulin or the pancreas failing to produce enough insulin. Unlike people with type 1 diabetes, those with type 2 can sometimes manage their condition with lifestyle changes and medication.

- **Gestational Diabetes:** This type of diabetes develops in some women during pregnancy and usually goes away after the baby is born. However, women who have had gestational diabetes are at an increased risk of developing type 2 diabetes later in life.Prediabetes: This is a condition where blood sugar levels are higher than normal, but not high enough to be diagnosed as diabetes. Without lifestyle changes, people with prediabetes are very likely to progress to type 2 diabetes.

If not well-managed, diabetes can lead to serious health complications, including heart disease, stroke, kidney disease, eye problems, dental disease, nerve damage, and foot problems. Therefore, it's important to maintain a healthy lifestyle, including regular exercise, a balanced diet, regular health check-ups, and adherence to prescribed medication or insulin therapy.

Dietary requirements for diabetes?

The dietary requirements for people with diabetes primarily aim at maintaining stable blood glucose levels, managing weight, preventing complications, and ensuring overall nutritional needs are met. Here are some key guidelines:

- **Carbohydrate Counting:** Carbohydrates have the most immediate impact on blood sugar levels. Therefore, it's crucial to understand how much carbohydrate is in each meal. This does not mean you need to eliminate carbs, but rather balance them in your diet and understand how they impact your blood sugar levels.

- **Healthy Fats**: Include heart-healthy omega-3 fatty acids in your diet, found in fatty fish, flaxseeds, and walnuts. Try to limit saturated fats and trans fats, which can raise your cholesterol levels.Fiber-Rich Foods: Consuming plenty of fiber can help regulate the body's blood sugar levels by slowing the rate at which sugar is absorbed into the bloodstream. Whole grains, legumes, fruits, vegetables, and nuts are excellent sources of dietary fiber.

- **Limit Sugary Drinks:** Sugary drinks like sodas, sweet teas, and fruit drinks can raise blood glucose levels quickly and can also add unnecessary calories.

- **Reduce Sodium Intake:** This can help prevent or manage high blood pressure, which is often a concern for individuals with diabetes.

- Remember, everyone's body responds differently to different types of foods and diets, so it's important to monitor blood glucose levels before and after meals to understand how your body responds to certain foods. Working with a registered dietitian can help you create a meal plan that fits your personal health goals, food preferences, and lifestyle.

What are the health benefits of following a diabetes diet?

Following a diabetes-friendly diet can offer numerous health benefits, not just for people with diabetes, but anyone looking to lead a healthier lifestyle. Here are some of the key benefits:

- **Better Blood Sugar Control:** A well-planned diabetes diet can help maintain stable blood sugar levels and prevent sudden spikes and drops, which are crucial for managing diabetes.
- **Weight Management:** Diabetes diets often emphasize portion control and nutritious food choices, which can help with weight loss and overall weight management. Maintaining a healthy weight can improve blood sugar control and has been shown to improve cardiovascular health.
- **Improved Energy Levels:** By ensuring a steady intake of complex carbohydrates and avoiding spikes and crashes in blood sugar, a diabetes diet can help maintain steady energy levels throughout the day.
- **Improved Heart Health:** A diabetes diet typically recommends reducing saturated and trans fats, sodium, and cholesterol, which can lower the risk of heart disease and stroke, common complications among people with diabetes.
- **Overall Nutritional Health:** A diabetes diet is a healthy eating plan that emphasizes fruits, vegetables, whole grains, and lean proteins. This not only helps manage diabetes but also ensures that you meet your overall nutritional needs.

Remember, every person with diabetes is unique, and dietary needs may vary. It's important to work with a healthcare provider or a dietitian to create a meal plan that suits your personal health goals, food preferences, and lifestyle.

Breakfast Recipes

Popcorn With Olive Oil

Servings: 14
Cooking Time: 10 Minutes
Ingredients:
- 1 tablespoon water
- ½ cup popcorn kernels
- 2 tablespoons extra-virgin olive oil
- ½ teaspoon salt
- ½ teaspoon pepper

Directions:
1. Heat Dutch oven over medium-high heat for 2 minutes. Add water and popcorn, cover, and cook, shaking frequently, until first few kernels begin to pop. Continue to cook, shaking vigorously, until popping slows to about 2 seconds between pops. Transfer popcorn to large serving bowl and toss with oil, salt, and pepper. Serve.

Nutrition Info:
- Info90 cal., 4g fat (0g sag. fat), 0mg chol, 170mg sod., 10g carb (0g sugars, 2g fiber), 1g pro.

Southwest Breakfast Pockets

Servings: 2
Cooking Time: 20 Minutes
Ingredients:
- 2 large eggs
- 2 large egg whites
- 1 teaspoon olive oil
- 1 small onion, chopped
- 1 garlic clove, minced
- 1/2 cup canned pinto beans, rinsed and drained
- 4 whole wheat pita pocket halves, warmed
- 1/4 cup salsa
- Sliced avocado, optional

Directions:
1. Whisk together eggs and egg whites. In a large nonstick skillet, heat oil over medium heat; saute onion until tender, 3-4 minutes. Add garlic; cook and stir 1 minute. Add eggs and beans; cook and stir until eggs are thickened and no liquid egg remains.
2. Spoon into pitas. Serve with salsa and, if desired, avocado.

Nutrition Info:
- Info339 cal., 9g fat (2g sat. fat), 186mg chol., 580mg sod., 47g carb. (4g sugars, 7g fiber), 19g pro.

Avocado And Bean Toast

Servings: 4
Cooking Time: 20 Minutes

Ingredients:
- 1 small red onion, halved and sliced thin
- ½ cup red wine vinegar
- ½ teaspoon red pepper flakes
- 4 ounces grape or cherry tomatoes, quartered
- 4 teaspoons extra-virgin olive oil
- Salt and pepper
- 1 (15-ounce) can no-salt-added black beans, rinsed
- ¼ cup boiling water
- ½ teaspoon grated lime zest plus 1 tablespoon juice
- 4 (2-ounce) slices rustic 100 percent whole-grain bread, toasted
- 1 ripe avocado, halved, pitted, and sliced thin
- ¼ cup fresh cilantro leaves

Directions:
1. Combine onion, vinegar, and pepper flakes in small bowl and let sit at room temperature for at least 20 minutes. (Onions can be refrigerated for up to 3 days.)
2. Combine tomatoes, 1 teaspoon oil, pinch salt, and pinch pepper in second bowl. Using potato masher in third bowl, mash beans, boiling water, lime zest and juice, ½ teaspoon salt, pinch pepper, and remaining 1 tablespoon oil to coarse paste, leaving some whole beans intact.
3. Spread mashed bean mixture evenly on toast and shingle avocado on top. Drain onions, then arrange on top of avocado along with tomatoes and cilantro. Serve.

Nutrition Info:
- Info350 cal., 15g fat (2g sag. fat), 0mg chol, 560mg sod., 42g carb (6g sugars, 12g fiber), 13g pro.

Sausage-egg Burritos

Servings: 6
Cooking Time: 20 Minutes

Ingredients:
- 1/2 pound bulk lean turkey breakfast sausage
- 3 large eggs
- 4 large egg whites
- 1 tablespoon olive oil
- 2 cups chopped fresh spinach
- 2 plum tomatoes, seeded and chopped
- 1 garlic clove, minced
- 1/4 teaspoon pepper
- 6 whole wheat tortillas (8 inches), warmed
- Salsa, optional

Directions:
1. In a large nonstick skillet coated with cooking spray, cook sausage over medium heat 4-6 minutes or until no longer pink, breaking into crumbles. Remove from pan.
2. In a small bowl, whisk eggs and egg whites until blended. In same pan, add eggs; cook and stir over medium heat until eggs are thickened and no liquid egg remains. Remove from pan; wipe skillet clean if necessary.
3. In a skillet, heat oil over medium-high heat. Add spinach, tomatoes and garlic; cook and stir for 2-3 minutes or until the spinach is wilted. Stir in sausage and eggs; heat through. Sprinkle mixture with pepper.
4. To serve, spoon 2/3 cup filling across center of each tortilla. Fold bottom and sides of tortilla over filling and roll up. If desired, serve with salsa.

Nutrition Info:
- Info258 cal., 10g fat (2g sat. fat), 134mg chol., 596mg sod., 24g carb. (1g sugars, 4g fiber), 20g pro.

Toasted Corn Salsa

Servings: 2
Cooking Time: 1 Hour
Ingredients:
- 4½ teaspoons extra-virgin olive oil
- 2 ears corn, kernels cut from cobs
- 1 red bell pepper, stemmed, seeded, and chopped fine
- ½ jalapeño chile, stemmed, seeded, and minced
- 1 scallion, sliced thin
- 2 garlic cloves, minced
- 2 tablespoons lime juice, plus extra for seasoning
- 2 tablespoons minced fresh cilantro
- ½ teaspoon ground cumin
- ¼ teaspoon salt
- ⅛ teaspoon pepper

Directions:
1. Heat 1½ teaspoons oil in 12-inch nonstick skillet over medium-high heat until shimmering. Add corn and cook, stirring occasionally, until golden brown, 6 to 8 minutes.
2. Transfer corn to medium serving bowl and stir in remaining 1 tablespoon oil, bell pepper, jalapeño, scallion, garlic, lime juice, cilantro, cumin, salt, and pepper. Cover and refrigerate until flavors meld, at least 1 hour or up to 2 days. Season with extra lime juice to taste before serving.

Nutrition Info:
- Info50 cal., 3g fat (0g sag. fat), 0mg chol, 75mg sod., 6g carb (2g sugars, 1g fiber), 1g pro.

Sweet Onion Frittata With Ham

Servings: 4
Cooking Time: 8 Minutes
Ingredients:
- 4 ounces extra-lean, low-sodium ham slices, chopped
- 1 cup thinly sliced Vidalia onion
- 1 1/2 cups egg substitute
- 1/3 cup shredded, reduced-fat, sharp cheddar cheese

Directions:
1. Place a medium nonstick skillet over medium-high heat until hot. Coat the skillet with nonstick cooking spray, add ham, and cook until beginning to lightly brown, about 2–3 minutes, stirring frequently. Remove from skillet and set aside on separate plate.
2. Reduce the heat to medium, coat the skillet with nonstick cooking spray, add onions, and cook 4 minutes or until beginning to turn golden, stirring frequently.
3. Reduce the heat to medium low, add ham to the onions, and cook 1 minute (this allows the flavors to blend and the skillet to cool slightly before the eggs are added). Pour egg substitute evenly over all, cover, and cook 8 minutes or until puffy and set.
4. Remove the skillet from the heat, sprinkle cheese evenly over all, cover, and let stand 3 minutes to melt the cheese and develop flavors.

Nutrition Info:
- Info110 cal., 2g fat (1g sag. fat), 20mg chol, 460mg sod., 6g carb (4g sugars, 0g fiber), 17g pro.

Breakfast Tacos

Servings: 2
Cooking Time: 10 minutes
Ingredients:
- 1 plum tomato, cored and chopped fine
- 1 shallot, minced
- ¼ cup fresh cilantro leaves
- 1 tablespoon minced jalapeño chile
- 1 tablespoon lime juice
- Salt
- 4 large eggs
- 2 tablespoons 1 percent low-fat milk
- 1 teaspoon canola oil
- 1 ounce cheddar cheese, shredded (¼ cup)
- 4 (6-inch) corn tortillas, warmed
- ½ avocado, sliced ¼ inch thick

Directions:
1. Combine tomato, shallot, 2 tablespoons cilantro, jalapeño, lime juice, and pinch salt in bowl; set pico de gallo aside for serving.
2. Beat eggs, milk, and pinch salt with fork in bowl until eggs are thoroughly combined and color is pure yellow; do not overbeat.
3. Heat oil in 10-inch nonstick skillet over medium-high heat until shimmering, swirling to coat pan. Add egg mixture and, using rubber spatula, constantly and firmly scrape along bottom and sides of skillet until eggs begin to clump and spatula just leaves trail on bottom of pan, 45 to 75 seconds. Reduce heat to low and gently but constantly fold eggs until clumped and just slightly wet, 30 to 60 seconds. Quickly fold in cheddar, then immediately transfer eggs to medium bowl.
4. Divide egg mixture between tortillas and top with pico de gallo, avocado, and remaining 2 tablespoons cilantro leaves. Serve immediately.

Nutrition Info:
- Info440 cal., 26g fat (7g sag. fat), 390mg chol, 430mg sod., 33g carb (4g sugars, 6g fiber), 20g pro.

Crunchy French Toast

Servings: 4
Cooking Time: 20 Minutes
Ingredients:
- 6 large eggs
- 1/3 cup fat-free milk
- 2 teaspoons vanilla extract
- 1/8 teaspoon salt
- 1 cup frosted cornflakes, crushed
- 1/2 cup old-fashioned oats
- 1/4 cup sliced almonds
- 8 slices whole wheat bread
- Maple syrup, optional

Directions:
1. In a shallow bowl, whisk eggs, milk, vanilla and salt until blended. In another shallow bowl, toss cornflakes with oats and almonds.
2. Heat a griddle coated with cooking spray over medium heat. Dip both sides of bread in egg mixture, then in cereal mixture, patting to help coating adhere. Place on griddle; toast 3-4 minutes on each side or until golden brown. If desired, serve with syrup.

Nutrition Info:
- Info335 cal., 11g fat (2g sat. fat), 196mg chol., 436mg sod., 43g carb. (8g sugars, 5g fiber), 17g pro.

Raspberry Peach Puff Pancake

Servings: 4
Cooking Time: 20 Minutes
Ingredients:
- 2 medium peaches, peeled and sliced
- 1/2 teaspoon sugar
- 1/2 cup fresh raspberries
- 1 tablespoon butter
- 3 large eggs, lightly beaten
- 1/2 cup fat-free milk
- 1/8 teaspoon salt
- 1/2 cup all-purpose flour
- 1/4 cup vanilla yogurt

Directions:
1. Preheat oven to 400°. In a small bowl, toss peaches with sugar; gently stir in raspberries.
2. Place butter in a 9-in. pie plate; heat in oven 2-3 minutes or until butter is melted. Meanwhile, in a small bowl, whisk eggs, milk and salt until blended; gradually whisk in in flour. Remove pie plate from the oven; tilt carefully, coating bottom and sides with butter. Immediately pour in egg mixture.
3. Bake 18-22 minutes or until puffed and browned. Remove pancake from the oven. Serve immediately with fruit mixture and yogurt.

Nutrition Info:
- Info199 cal., 7g fat (3g sat. fat), 149mg chol., 173mg sod., 25g carb. (11g sugars, 3g fiber), 9g pro.

Marinated Artichokes

Servings: 8
Cooking Time: 20 Minutes
Ingredients:
- 2 lemons
- 2½ cups extra-virgin olive oil
- 3 pounds baby artichokes (3 ounces each)
- 8 garlic cloves (6 peeled and smashed, 2 minced)
- ¼ teaspoon red pepper flakes
- 2 sprigs fresh thyme
- ½ teaspoon salt
- ¼ teaspoon pepper
- 2 tablespoons minced fresh mint

Directions:
1. Using vegetable peeler, remove three 2-inch strips zest from 1 lemon. Grate ½ teaspoon zest from second lemon and set aside. Halve and juice lemons to yield ¼ cup juice, reserving spent lemon halves.
2. Combine oil and lemon zest strips in large saucepan. Working with 1 artichoke at a time, cut top quarter off each, snap off outer leaves, and trim away dark parts. Peel and trim stem, then cut artichoke in half lengthwise (quarter artichoke if large). Rub each artichoke half with spent lemon half and place in saucepan.
3. Add smashed garlic, pepper flakes, thyme sprigs, salt, and pepper to oil in saucepan and bring to rapid simmer over high heat. Reduce heat to medium-low and simmer, stirring occasionally to submerge all artichokes, until artichokes can be pierced with fork but are still firm, about 5 minutes. Remove from heat, cover, and let sit until artichokes are fork-tender and fully cooked, about 20 minutes.
4. Transfer artichokes and ¼ cup oil to serving bowl and gently stir in ½ teaspoon reserved grated lemon zest, ¼ cup reserved lemon juice, and minced garlic. Discard remaining oil or reserve for another use. Let artichokes cool to room temperature. Sprinkle with mint and serve. (Artichokes and reserved oil can be refrigerated separately for up to 4 days.)

Nutrition Info:
- Info100 cal., 7g fat (1g sag. fat), 0mg chol, 135mg sod., 8g carb (1g sugars, 4g fiber), 2g pro.

Cheesy Baked Grits

Servings: 10
Cooking Time: 60 Minutes
Ingredients:
- 1 tablespoon unsalted butter
- 1 onion, chopped fine
- 1 teaspoon salt
- 4½ cups water
- 1½ cups 1 percent low-fat milk
- ¾ teaspoon hot sauce
- 1½ cups old-fashioned grits
- 4 ounces extra-sharp cheddar cheese, shredded (1 cup)
- 4 large eggs, lightly beaten
- ¼ teaspoon pepper

Directions:
1. Adjust oven rack to lower-middle position and heat oven to 350 degrees. Lightly spray 13 by 9-inch baking dish with canola oil spray. Melt butter in large saucepan over medium heat. Add onion and salt and cook until softened, about 5 minutes. Stir in water, milk, and hot sauce and bring to boil.
2. Pour grits into boiling liquid in very slow stream while whisking constantly in circular motion to prevent clumping. Reduce heat to low, cover, and cook, stirring often and vigorously (make sure to scrape corners of pot), until grits are thick and creamy, 10 to 15 minutes.
3. Off heat, whisk in ½ cup cheddar, eggs, and pepper. Pour mixture into prepared dish, smooth top, and sprinkle with remaining ½ cup cheddar. Bake until top is browned and grits are hot, 35 to 45 minutes. Let cool for 10 minutes before serving.

Nutrition Info:
- Info190 cal., 8g fat (4g sag. fat), 90mg chol, 360mg sod., 22g carb (3g sugars, 2g fiber), 7g pro.

Kale Chips

Servings: 8
Cooking Time: 60 Minutes
Ingredients:
- 12 ounces Lacinato kale, stemmed and torn into 3-inch pieces
- 1 tablespoon extra-virgin olive oil
- ½ teaspoon kosher salt

Directions:
1. Adjust oven racks to upper-middle and lower-middle positions and heat oven to 200 degrees. Set wire racks in 2 rimmed baking sheets. Dry kale thoroughly between dish towels, transfer to large bowl, and toss with oil and salt.
2. Arrange kale on prepared racks, making sure leaves overlap as little as possible. Bake kale until very crisp, 45 to 60 minutes, switching and rotating sheets halfway through baking. Let kale chips cool completely before serving. (Kale chips can be stored in paper towel–lined airtight container for up to 1 day.)

Nutrition Info:
- Info60 cal., 4g fat (0g sag. fat), 0mg chol, 160mg sod., 5g carb (1g sugars, 2g fiber), 3g pro.

Crispy Polenta Squares With Olives And Sun-dried Tomatoes

Servings: 24
Cooking Time: x

Ingredients:

- 2 tablespoons plus 1 teaspoon extra-virgin olive oil
- 4 garlic cloves, minced
- ½ teaspoon minced fresh rosemary
- 2 cups water
- ½ teaspoon salt
- ½ cup instant polenta
- ¼ teaspoon pepper
- ⅓ cup pitted kalamata olives, chopped fine
- ⅓ cup oil-packed sun-dried tomatoes, patted dry and chopped fine
- ½ teaspoon red wine vinegar
- 1 tablespoon minced fresh basil

Directions:

1. Line 8½ by 4½-inch loaf pan with parchment paper and lightly coat with canola oil spray. Cook 4 teaspoons oil and three-quarters of garlic in 8-inch nonstick skillet over low heat, stirring often, until garlic is golden and fragrant, about 10 minutes. Off heat, stir in rosemary; set aside.
2. Bring water to boil in large saucepan. Reduce heat to low and stir in salt. Slowly add polenta while whisking constantly in circular motion to prevent clumping. Continue to cook, stirring often, until polenta is soft and smooth, 3 to 5 minutes. Off heat, stir in oil-garlic mixture and ⅛ teaspoon pepper.
3. Pour polenta into prepared pan, smooth top, and let cool to room temperature, about 2 hours. Wrap pan tightly in plastic wrap and refrigerate until polenta is very firm, at least 2 hours or up to 24 hours.
4. Combine olives, tomatoes, vinegar, remaining 1 tablespoon oil, remaining garlic, and remaining ⅛ teaspoon pepper in bowl; set aside.
5. Run small knife around edge of polenta, then flip onto cutting board; discard parchment. Trim polenta loaf as needed to create uniform edges. Cut loaf in half lengthwise, then cut each strip crosswise into 6 pieces. Slice polenta pieces in half to form ¼-inch-thick squares. (You should have 24 squares.)
6. Adjust oven rack 3 inches from broiler element. (If necessary, set overturned rimmed baking sheet on oven rack to get closer to broiler element.) Place rimmed baking sheet on rack and heat broiler for 10 minutes. Carefully remove sheet from oven. Spray canola oil evenly on hot sheet and arrange squares in single layer. Broil polenta until spotty brown and crisp, 8 to 10 minutes. Transfer polenta to serving platter, top each square with olive mixture, sprinkle with basil, and serve.

Nutrition Info:

- Info90 cal., 5g fat (0g sag. fat), 0mg chol, 180mg sod., 10g carb (0g sugars, 1g fiber), 1g pro.

Egg & Hash Brown Breakfast Cups

Servings: 2
Cooking Time: 30 Minutes

Ingredients:

- 3 uncooked turkey breakfast sausage links (1 ounce each), casings removed
- 3 tablespoons chopped green pepper
- 2 tablespoons chopped onion
- 1/2 cup frozen cubed hash brown potatoes
- 1/3 cup fat-free milk
- 1/4 cup egg substitute
- 3 tablespoons reduced-fat biscuit/baking mix
- 1/8 teaspoon pepper
- 2 tablespoons shredded reduced-fat cheddar cheese

Directions:

1. Preheat oven to 400°. In a nonstick skillet coated with cooking spray, cook and stir sausage with green pepper and onion over medium heat until no longer pink, breaking sausage into small pieces. Stir in potatoes. Divide among four muffin cups coated with cooking spray.
2. Whisk together milk, egg substitute, baking mix and pepper; pour into cups. Sprinkle with cheese. Bake until a knife inserted in center comes out clean, 13-15 minutes.

Nutrition Info:

- Info158 cal., 5g fat (2g sat. fat), 28mg chol., 435mg sod., 15g carb. (4g sugars, 1g fiber), 13g pro.

Appetizers And Snacks Recipes

Zesty Lemony Shrimp

Servings: 8
Cooking Time: 7–10 Minutes
Ingredients:
- 12 ounces peeled raw medium shrimp, fresh, or frozen and thawed
- 2 tablespoons Worcestershire sauce
- 1 teaspoon lemon zest
- 3 tablespoons lemon juice
- 2 tablespoons no-trans-fat margarine (35% vegetable oil)
- 1 tablespoon finely chopped fresh parsley (optional)

Directions:
1. Place a large nonstick skillet over medium heat until hot. Add the shrimp, Worcestershire sauce, lemon zest, and lemon juice to the skillet. Cook 5 minutes or until shrimp is opaque in center, stirring frequently.
2. Using a slotted spoon, remove the shrimp and set aside in serving bowl. Increase the heat to medium high, add the margarine, bring to a boil, and continue to boil 2 minutes or until the liquid measures 1/4 cup, stirring constantly.
3. Pour the sauce over the shrimp and sprinkle with 1 tablespoon finely chopped parsley, if desired. Serve with wooden toothpicks.

Nutrition Info:
- Info50 cal., 0g fat (0g sag. fat), 70mg chol, 95mg sod., 1g carb (1g sugars, 0g fiber), 9g pro.

Avocado Endive Boats

Servings: 2
Cooking Time: 45 Minutes
Ingredients:
- 1 jar (12 ounces) roasted sweet red peppers, drained and finely chopped
- 1 cup finely chopped fennel bulb
- 1/4 cup sliced ripe olives, finely chopped
- 2 tablespoons olive oil
- 1 tablespoon minced fresh cilantro
- 1/2 teaspoon salt, divided
- 1/2 teaspoon pepper, divided
- 2 medium ripe avocados, peeled and pitted
- 3 tablespoons lime juice
- 2 tablespoons diced jalapeno pepper
- 1 green onion, finely chopped
- 1 garlic clove, minced
- 1/2 teaspoon ground cumin
- 1/4 teaspoon hot pepper sauce
- 2 plum tomatoes, chopppped
- 30 endive leaves
- Chopped fennel fronds

Directions:
1. In a small bowl, combine first five ingredients; stir in 1/4 teaspoon each salt and pepper.
2. In another bowl, mash avocados with a fork. Stir in next six ingredients and the remaining salt and pepper. Stir in tomatoes.
3. Spoon about 1 tablespoon avocado mixture onto each endive leaf; top each with about 1 tablespoon pepper mixture. Sprinkle with fennel fronds.

Nutrition Info:
- Info43 cal., 3g fat (0 sat. fat), 0 chol., 109mg sod., 4g carb. (1g sugars, 3g fiber), 1g pro.

Dilled Chex Toss

Servings: 18
Cooking Time: 30 Minutes
Ingredients:
- 6 cups multi-grain or Wheat Chex cereal
- 4-ounce packet ranch salad dressing mix
- 1 tablespoon dried dill
- 2 tablespoons extra virgin olive oil

Directions:
1. Preheat the oven to 175°F.
2. Place the cereal, dressing mix, and dill in a large zippered plastic bag. Seal and shake gently to blend well.
3. Place the mixture on a large rimmed baking sheet or jelly roll pan, drizzle the oil evenly over all, and stir thoroughly to blend. Spread out in a single layer and bake 30 minutes or until browned lightly, stirring once.

Nutrition Info:
- Info50 cal., 1g fat (0g sag. fat), 0mg chol, 200mg sod., 8g carb (1g sugars, 1g fiber), 1g pro.

Bleu Cheese'd Pears

Servings: 4
Cooking Time: 5 Minutes
Ingredients:
- 2 ounces fat-free cream cheese
- 3 1/2 tablespoons crumbled bleu cheese
- 2 medium firm pears, halved, cored, and sliced into 20 slices

Directions:
1. In a small bowl, microwave the cheeses on HIGH for 10 seconds to soften. Use a rubber spatula to blend well.
2. Top each pear slice with 3/4 teaspoon cheese.
3. To prevent the pear slices from discoloring, toss them with a tablespoon of orange, pineapple, or lemon juice. Shake off the excess liquid before topping them with cheese.

Nutrition Info:
- Info90 cal., 2g fat (1g sag. fat), 10mg chol, 190mg sod., 14g carb (9g sugars, 3g fiber), 4g pro.

Chicken, Mango & Blue Cheese Tortillas

Servings: 16
Cooking Time: 30 Minutes
Ingredients:
- 1 boneless skinless chicken breast (8 ounces)
- 1 teaspoon blackened seasoning
- 3/4 cup (6 ounces) plain yogurt
- 1 1/2 teaspoons grated lime peel
- 2 tablespoons lime juice
- 1/4 teaspoon salt
- 1/8 teaspoon pepper
- 1 cup finely chopped peeled mango
- 1/3 cup finely chopped red onion
- 4 flour tortillas (8 inches)
- 1/2 cup crumbled blue cheese
- 2 tablespoons minced fresh cilantro

Directions:
1. Lightly oil grill rack with cooking oil. Sprinkle the chicken with blackened seasoning; grill, covered, over medium heat 6-8 minutes on each side or until a thermometer reads 165°.
2. In a bowl, mix yogurt, lime peel, lime juice, salt and pepper. Cool chicken slightly; finely chop and transfer to a small bowl. Stir in mango and onion.
3. Grill tortillas, uncovered, over medium heat 2-3 minutes, until puffed. Turn; top with chicken mixture and blue cheese. Grill, covered, 2-3 minutes, until bottoms are lightly browned. Drizzle with yogurt mixture; sprinkle with cilantro. Cut each into four wedges.

Nutrition Info:
- Info85 cal., 3g fat (1g sat. fat), 12mg chol., 165mg sod., 10g carb. (2g sugars, 1g fiber), 5g pro.

Raisin & Hummus Pita Wedges

Servings: 8
Cooking Time: 15 Minutes
Ingredients:
- 1/4 cup golden raisins
- 1 tablespoon chopped dates
- 1/2 cup boiling water
- 2 whole wheat pita breads (6 inches)
- 2/3 cup hummus
- Snipped fresh dill or dill weed, optional

Directions:
1. Place raisins and dates in a small bowl. Cover with boiling water; let stand for 5 minutes. Drain well.
2. Cut each pita into four wedges. Spread with hummus; top with raisins, dates and, if desired, dill.

Nutrition Info:
- Info91 cal., 2g fat (0 sat. fat), 0 chol., 156mg sod., 16g carb. (4g sugars, 3g fiber), 3g pro.

Roasted Red Pepper Tapenade

Servings: 2
Cooking Time: 15 Minutes
Ingredients:
- 3 garlic cloves, peeled
- 2 cups roasted sweet red peppers, drained
- 1/2 cup blanched almonds
- 1/3 cup tomato paste
- 2 tablespoons olive oil
- 1/4 teaspoon salt
- 1/4 teaspoon pepper
- Minced fresh basil
- Toasted French bread baguette slices or water crackers

Directions:
1. In a small saucepan, bring 2 cups water to a boil. Add garlic; cook, uncovered, 6-8 minutes or just until tender. Drain and pat dry. Place red peppers, almonds, tomato paste, oil, garlic, salt and pepper in a small food processor; process until blended. Transfer to a small bowl. Refrigerate at least 4 hours to allow flavors to blend.
2. Sprinkle with basil. Serve with baguette slices.

Nutrition Info:
- Info58 cal., 4g fat (0 sat. fat), 0 chol., 152mg sod., 3g carb. (2g sugars, 1g fiber), 1g pro.

Crostini With Kalamata Tomato

Servings: 4
Cooking Time: 10 Minutes
Ingredients:
- 4 ounces multigrain baguette bread, cut in 12 slices (about 1/4 inch thick)
- 1 small tomato, finely chopped
- 9 small kalamata olives, pitted and finely chopped
- 2 tablespoons chopped fresh basil

Directions:
1. Preheat the oven to 350°F.
2. Arrange the bread slices on a baking sheet and bake 10 minutes or until just golden on the edges. Remove from the heat and cool completely.
3. Meanwhile, stir the remaining ingredients together in a small bowl. Spread 1 tablespoon of the mixture on each bread slice.

Nutrition Info:
- Info90 cal., 2g fat (0g sag. fat), 0mg chol, 220mg sod., 16g carb (2g sugars, 1g fiber), 3g pro.

Blueberry Salsa

Servings: 1
Cooking Time: 15 Minutes
Ingredients:
- 1 1/2 cups fresh blueberries
- 1/4 cup chopped sweet red pepper
- 2 green onions, finely chopped
- 2 tablespoons minced seeded jalapeno pepper
- 2 tablespoons lemon juice
- 1 to 2 tablespoons minced fresh cilantro
- 1 1/2 teaspoons sugar
- 1/4 teaspoon salt
- Dash of pepper

Directions:
1. Place blueberries in a food processor; pulse five times or until coarsely chopped. Transfer to a small bowl; stir in remaining ingredients. Refrigerate until serving.

Nutrition Info:
- Info30 cal., 0 fat (0 sat. fat), 0 chol., 100mg sod., 8g carb. (5g sugars, 1g fiber), 0 pro.

Garden-fresh Wraps

Servings: 8
Cooking Time: 20 Minutes
Ingredients:
- 1 medium ear sweet corn
- 1 medium cucumber, chopped
- 1 cup shredded cabbage
- 1 medium tomato, chopped
- 1 small red onion, chopped
- 1 jalapeno pepper, seeded and minced
- 1 tablespoon minced fresh basil
- 1 tablespoon minced fresh cilantro
- 1 tablespoon minced fresh mint
- 1/3 cup Thai chili sauce
- 3 tablespoons rice vinegar
- 2 teaspoons reduced-sodium soy sauce
- 2 teaspoons creamy peanut butter
- 8 Bibb or Boston lettuce leaves

Directions:
1. Cut corn from cob and place in a large bowl. Add cucumber, cabbage, tomato, onion, jalapeno and herbs.
2. Whisk together chili sauce, vinegar, soy sauce and peanut butter. Pour over vegetable mixture; toss to coat. Let stand 20 minutes.
3. Using a slotted spoon, place 1/2 cup salad in each lettuce leaf. Fold lettuce over filling.

Nutrition Info:
- Info64 cal., 1g fat (0 sat. fat), 0 chol., 319mg sod., 13g carb. (10g sugars, 2g fiber), 2g pro.

Baked Pot Stickers With Dipping Sauce

Servings: 4
Cooking Time: 15 Minutes
Ingredients:
- 2 cups finely chopped cooked chicken breast
- 1 can (8 ounces) water chestnuts, drained and chopped
- 4 green onions, thinly sliced
- 1/4 cup shredded carrots
- 1/4 cup reduced-fat mayonnaise
- 1 large egg white
- 1 tablespoon reduced-sodium soy sauce
- 1 garlic clove, minced
- 1 teaspoon grated fresh gingerroot
- 48 wonton wrappers
- Cooking spray
- SAUCE
- 1/2 cup jalapeno pepper jelly
- 1/4 cup rice vinegar
- 2 tablespoons reduced-sodium soy sauce

Directions:
1. Preheat the oven to 425°. In a large bowl, combine the first nine ingredients. Place 2 teaspoons of filling in the center of a wonton wrapper. Cover the rest of wrappers with a damp paper towel until ready to use.
2. Moisten filled wrapper edges with water. Fold edge over filling and roll to form a log; twist ends to seal. Repeat with remaining wrappers and filling.
3. Place pot stickers on a baking sheet coated with cooking spray; spritz each with cooking spray. Bake 12-15 minutes or until edges are golden brown.
4. Meanwhile, place jelly in a small microwave-safe bowl; microwave, covered, on high until melted. Stir in vinegar and soy sauce. Serve sauce with pot stickers.

Nutrition Info:
- Info52 cal., 1g fat (0 sat. fat), 6mg chol., 101mg sod., 8g carb. (2g sugars, 0 fiber), 3g pro.

Minutesi Feta Pizzas

Servings: 4
Cooking Time: 20 Minutes
Ingredients:
- 2 whole wheat English muffins, split and toasted
- 2 tablespoons reduced-fat cream cheese
- 4 teaspoons prepared pesto
- 1/2 cup thinly sliced red onion
- 1/4 cup crumbled feta cheese

Directions:
1. Preheat oven to 425°. Place muffins on a baking sheet.
2. Mix cream cheese and pesto; spread over muffins. Top with onion and feta cheese. Bake until lightly browned, 6-8 minutes.

Nutrition Info:
- Info136 cal., 6g fat (3g sat. fat), 11mg chol., 294mg sod., 16g carb. (4g sugars, 3g fiber), 6g pro.

Meatballs In Cherry Sauce

Servings: 3
Cooking Time: 15 Minutes
Ingredients:
- 1 cup seasoned bread crumbs
- 1 small onion, chopped
- 1 large egg, lightly beaten
- 3 garlic cloves, minced
- 1 teaspoon salt
- 1/2 teaspoon pepper
- 1 pound lean ground beef (90% lean)
- 1 pound ground pork
- SAUCE
- 1 can (21 ounces) cherry pie filling
- 1/3 cup sherry or chicken broth
- 1/3 cup cider vinegar
- 1/4 cup steak sauce
- 2 tablespoons brown sugar
- 2 tablespoons reduced-sodium soy sauce
- 1 teaspoon honey

Directions:
1. Preheat oven to 400°. In a large bowl, combine the first six ingredients. Add the beef and pork; mix lightly but thoroughly. Shape into 1-in. balls. Place on a greased rack in a shallow baking pan. Bake for 11-13 minutes or until cooked through. Drain on paper towels.
2. In a saucepan, combine the sauce ingredients. Bring to a boil over medium heat, stirring constantly. Reduce heat; simmer, uncovered, 2-3 minutes or until thickened. Add meatballs; heat through.

Nutrition Info:
- Info76 cal., 3g fat (1g sat. fat), 19mg chol., 169mg sod., 7g carb. (5g sugars, 0 fiber), 5g pro.

Lime'd Blueberries

Servings: 6
Cooking Time: 5 Minutes
Ingredients:
- 2 cups frozen unsweetened blueberries, partially thawed
- 1/4 cup frozen grape juice concentrate
- 1 1/2 tablespoons lime juice

Directions:
1. Place all ingredients in a medium bowl and toss gently.
2. Serve immediately for peak flavor and texture.

Nutrition Info:
- Info50 cal., 0g fat (0g sag. fat), 0mg chol, 5mg sod., 13g carb (11g sugars, 1g fiber), 0g pro.

Poultry Recipes

Southwest-style Shepherd's Pie

Servings: 6
Cooking Time: 25 Minutes
Ingredients:
- 1 1/4 pounds lean ground turkey
- 1 small onion, chopped
- 2 garlic cloves, minced
- 1/2 teaspoon salt, divided
- 1 can (14 3/4 ounces) cream-style corn
- 1 can (4 ounces) chopped green chilies
- 1 to 2 tablespoons chipotle hot pepper sauce, optional
- 2 2/3 cups water
- 2 tablespoons butter
- 2 tablespoons half-and-half cream
- 1/2 teaspoon pepper
- 2 cups mashed potato flakes

Directions:
1. Preheat oven to 425°. In a large skillet, cook turkey, onion, garlic and 1/4 teaspoon salt over medium heat 8-10 minutes or until turkey is no longer pink and onion is tender, breaking up turkey into crumbles. Stir in corn, green chilies and, if desired, pepper sauce. Transfer to a greased 8-in. square baking dish.
2. Meanwhile, in a saucepan, bring the water, butter, cream, pepper and remaining salt to a boil. Remove from heat. Stir in potato flakes. Spoon over turkey mixture, spreading to cover. Bake for 25-30 minutes or until bubbly and potatoes are light brown.

Nutrition Info:
- Info312 cal., 12g fat (5g sat. fat), 78mg chol., 583mg sod., 31g carb. (4g sugars, 3g fiber), 22g pro.

Turkey-thyme Stuffed Peppers

Servings: 4
Cooking Time: 10 Minutes
Ingredients:
- 1 pound lean ground turkey
- 1 medium onion, finely chopped
- 3 garlic cloves, minced
- 1/2 teaspoon dried thyme
- 1/4 teaspoon salt
- 1/4 teaspoon dried rosemary, crushed
- 1/8 teaspoon pepper
- 1 can (14 1/2 ounces) diced tomatoes, undrained
- 1 package (8.8 ounces) ready-to-serve brown rice
- 1/2 cup seasoned bread crumbs
- 4 medium sweet yellow or orange peppers
- 1/4 cup shredded part-skim mozzarella cheese

Directions:
1. In a large skillet, cook turkey and onion over medium heat 8-10 minutes or until the turkey is no longer pink and onion is tender, breaking up turkey into crumbles. Add garlic and seasonings; cook 1 minute longer. Stir in tomatoes, rice and bread crumbs.
2. Cut sweet peppers lengthwise in half; remove seeds. Arrange pepper halves in a 13x9-in. microwave-safe dish; fill with turkey mixture. Sprinkle with cheese. Microwave, covered, on high for 7-9 minutes or until peppers are crisp-tender.

Nutrition Info:
- Info423 cal., 13g fat (3g sat. fat), 82mg chol., 670mg sod., 43g carb. (10g sugars, 6g fiber), 31g pro.

Sausage Orecchiette Pasta

Servings: 6
Cooking Time: 25 Minutes
Ingredients:
- 4 cups uncooked orecchiette or small tube pasta
- 1 package (19 1/2 ounces) Italian turkey sausage links, casings removed
- 3 garlic cloves, minced
- 1 cup white wine or chicken broth
- 4 cups small fresh broccoli florets
- 1 can (14 1/2 ounces) diced tomatoes, drained
- 1/3 cup grated or shredded Parmesan cheese

Directions:
1. Cook pasta according to package directions. Meanwhile, in a large skillet, cook the sausage over medium heat for 6-8 minutes or until no longer pink, breaking into crumbles. Add garlic; cook 1 minute longer. Add the wine, stirring to loosen browned bits from pan. Bring the mixture to a boil; cook 1-2 minutes or until liquid is reduced by half.
2. Stir in the broccoli and tomatoes. Reduce heat and simmer, covered, 4-6 minutes or until broccoli is crisp-tender. Drain pasta; add to skillet and toss to coat. Serve with cheese.

Nutrition Info:
- Info363 cal., 8g fat (2g sat. fat), 38mg chol., 571mg sod., 48g carb. (4g sugars, 5g fiber), 20g pro.

Country Roast Chicken With Lemony Au Jus

Servings: 6
Cooking Time: 1 Hour And 20 Minutes
Ingredients:
- 3 1/2-pound roasting chicken, rinsed and patted dry, including the cavity
- 2 medium lemons, quartered
- 3/4 teaspoon poultry seasoning
- 3/4 teaspoon garlic powder
- 3/4 teaspoon salt
- 1/4 teaspoon black pepper
- 2 cups water

Directions:
1. Preheat the oven to 425°F.
2. Coat a broiler rack and pan with nonstick cooking spray. Place the chicken on the rack. Squeeze the lemons evenly over the chicken and place the lemon rinds in the cavity of the chicken.
3. Combine the poultry seasoning, garlic powder, salt, and pepper in a small bowl. Blend well and sprinkle evenly over the chicken. Place the chicken in the oven, pour the water through the slits of the broiler pan, and cook 30 minutes.
4. Reduce the heat to 375°F and cook 50–55 minutes or until a meat thermometer reaches 180°F. Remove the chicken from the oven and let it stand on the broiler rack for 10 minutes.
5. Place the chicken on a cutting board. Carefully pour the pan drippings into a grease separator or a plastic zippered bag. Freeze the drippings for 10 minutes to separate the grease.
6. Remove the grease from the separator or bag, pour drippings into a glass dish, and heat in the microwave on HIGH for 30 seconds. Slice the chicken, discarding the skin, and serve with the drippings.

Nutrition Info:
- Info160 cal., 6g fat (1g sag. fat), 75mg chol, 220mg sod., 1g carb (0g sugars, 0g fiber), 25g pro.

Avocado And Green Chili Chicken

Servings: 4
Cooking Time: 22 Minutes
Ingredients:
- 4 (4 ounces each) boneless, skinless chicken breast, flattened to 1/2-inch thickness
- 1 (4-ounce) can chopped mild green chilies
- 1 ripe medium avocado, chopped
- 1 lime, halved

Directions:
1. Preheat oven to 400°F.
2. Place chicken in an 11 × 7-inch baking pan, squeeze half of the lime over all. Spoon green chilies on top of each breast and spread over all. Bake, uncovered, 22–25 minutes or until chicken is no longer pink in center.
3. Top with avocado, squeeze remaining lime half over all, and sprinkle evenly with 1/4 teaspoon salt and 1/4 teaspoon pepper.

Nutrition Info:
- Info200 cal., 8g fat (1g sag. fat), 85mg chol, 310mg sod., 6g carb (1g sugars, 3g fiber), 27g pro.

Braised Chicken Breasts With Chickpeas And Chermoula

Servings: 4
Cooking Time: 20 Minutes
Ingredients:
- 1½ cups fresh cilantro leaves
- 6 tablespoons extra-virgin olive oil
- 3 tablespoons lemon juice, plus lemon wedges for serving
- 4 garlic cloves, minced
- 1 teaspoon ground cumin
- 1 teaspoon paprika
- ¼ teaspoon cayenne pepper
- Salt and pepper
- 2 (12-ounce) bone-in split chicken breasts, trimmed of all visible fat and halved crosswise
- 2 fennel bulbs, 2 tablespoons fronds minced, stalks discarded, bulbs halved, cored, and sliced thin
- ¾ cup unsalted chicken broth
- 2 (15-ounce) cans no-salt-added chickpeas, rinsed

Directions:
1. Process cilantro, ¼ cup oil, lemon juice, garlic, cumin, paprika, cayenne, and ¼ teaspoon salt in food processor until finely ground, about 1 minute, scraping down sides of bowl as needed. Transfer chermoula to bowl and set aside for serving.
2. Pound chicken breast pieces to uniform thickness as needed, pat dry with paper towels, and season with ¼ teaspoon salt and ¼ teaspoon pepper.
3. Heat 1 tablespoon oil in Dutch oven over medium-high heat until just smoking. Cook breast pieces skin side down in pot until well browned, 4 to 6 minutes; transfer to plate.
4. Heat remaining 1 tablespoon oil in now-empty pot over medium heat until shimmering. Add fennel and cook until softened, about 5 minutes. Stir in broth, scraping up any browned bits. Stir in chickpeas and bring to simmer. Nestle chicken pieces into pot along with any accumulated juices. Reduce heat to medium-low, cover, and cook until chicken registers 160 degrees, 15 to 20 minutes.
5. Transfer chicken to plate and discard skin. Stir fennel fronds and 1 tablespoon chermoula into chickpea mixture. Top individual portions of chicken and chickpea mixture evenly with remaining chermoula. Serve with lemon wedges.

Nutrition Info:
- Info550 cal., 26g fat (4g sag. fat), 100mg chol, 480mg sod., 35g carb (6g sugars, 10g fiber), 41g pro.

Baked Chicken Chalupas

Servings: 6
Cooking Time: 15 Minutes

Ingredients:
- 6 corn tortillas (6 inches)
- 2 teaspoons olive oil
- 3/4 cup shredded part-skim mozzarella cheese
- 2 cups chopped cooked chicken breast
- 1 can (14 1/2 ounces) diced tomatoes with mild green chilies, undrained
- 1 teaspoon garlic powder
- 1 teaspoon onion powder
- 1 teaspoon ground cumin
- 1/4 teaspoon salt
- 1/4 teaspoon pepper
- 1/2 cup finely shredded cabbage

Directions:
1. Preheat oven to 350°. Place the tortillas on an ungreased baking sheet. Brush each tortilla with oil; sprinkle with mozzarella cheese.
2. Place the chicken, tomatoes and seasonings in a large skillet; cook and stir over medium heat 6-8 minutes or until most of the liquid is evaporated. Spoon over tortillas. Bake 15-18 minutes or until tortillas are crisp and cheese is melted. Top with cabbage.

Nutrition Info:
- Info206 cal., 6g fat (2g sat. fat), 45mg chol., 400mg sod., 17g carb. (3g sugars, 3g fiber), 19g pro.

Pan-seared Chicken Breasts With Leek And White Wine Pan Sauce

Servings: 4
Cooking Time: 20 Minutes

Ingredients:
- CHICKEN
- 4 (6-ounce) boneless, skinless chicken breasts, trimmed of all visible fat
- Salt and pepper
- 1 tablespoon canola oil
- PAN SAUCE
- 1 leek, white and light green parts only, halved lengthwise, sliced ¼ inch thick, and washed thoroughly
- Salt and pepper
- 1 teaspoon all-purpose flour
- ¾ cup unsalted chicken broth
- ½ cup dry white wine or dry vermouth
- 1 tablespoon unsalted butter, chilled
- 2 teaspoons chopped fresh tarragon
- 1 teaspoon whole-grain mustard

Directions:
1. FOR THE CHICKEN Pound chicken breasts to uniform thickness as needed. Pat dry with paper towels and sprinkle with ¼ teaspoon salt and ⅛ teaspoon pepper. Heat oil in 12-inch skillet over medium-high heat until just smoking. Cook breasts, turning as needed, until well browned and register 160 degrees, about 10 minutes. Transfer breasts to plate, tent with aluminum foil, and let rest while preparing sauce.
2. FOR THE PAN SAUCE Pour off all but 2 teaspoons fat from skillet. (If necessary, add oil to equal 2 teaspoons.) Add leek and ⅛ teaspoon salt and cook over medium heat until softened and lightly browned, 5 to 7 minutes. Stir in flour and cook for 1 minute. Slowly whisk in broth and wine, scraping up any browned bits and smoothing out any lumps. Bring to simmer and cook sauce until thickened and measures about ¾ cup, 3 to 5 minutes.
3. Off heat, whisk in butter until combined, then whisk in tarragon, mustard, and any accumulated chicken juices. Season with pepper to taste. Spoon sauce evenly over each breast before serving.

Nutrition Info:
- Info310 cal., 11g fat (3g sag. fat), 130mg chol, 350mg sod., 5g carb (1g sugars, 1g fiber), 39g pro.

Sausage And Farro Mushrooms

Servings: 4
Cooking Time: 20 Minutes
Ingredients:
- 1/2 cup dry pearled farro
- 2 (3.9 ounces each) Italian turkey sausage links, removed from casing, such as Jennie-o
- 8 portabella mushroom caps, stems removed, caps wiped with damp cloth
- 2 tablespoons crumbled reduced-fat blue cheese

Directions:
1. Preheat broiler. Coat both sides of the mushrooms with cooking spray, place on a foil-lined baking sheet, and broil 5 minutes on each side or until tender.
2. Meanwhile, heat a large nonstick skillet over medium-high heat, add sausage, and cook 3 minutes or until browned, breaking up larger pieces while cooking. Set aside on separate plate.
3. Add 2 cups water and the farro to any pan residue in skillet, bring to a boil, reduce heat to medium-low, cover, and simmer 15 minutes or until slightly "chewy." Stir in the sausage and cheese; cook, uncovered, for 2 minutes to thicken slightly. Spoon equal amounts into each mushroom cap and sprinkle with black pepper.

Nutrition Info:
- Info200 cal., 6g fat (1g sag. fat), 30mg chol, 390mg sod., 23g carb (2g sugars, 3g fiber), 16g pro.

Quick & Easy Turkey Sloppy Joes

Servings: 8
Cooking Time: 30 Minutes
Ingredients:
- 1 pound lean ground turkey
- 1 large red onion, chopped
- 1 large green pepper, chopped
- 1 can (8 ounces) tomato sauce
- 1/2 cup barbecue sauce
- 1 teaspoon dried oregano
- 1 teaspoon ground cumin
- 1 teaspoon chili powder
- 1/4 teaspoon salt
- 8 hamburger buns, split

Directions:
1. In a large skillet, cook turkey, onion and pepper over medium heat for 6-8 minutes or until turkey is no longer pink and vegetables are tender, breaking up turkey into crumbles.
2. Stir in tomato sauce, barbecue sauce and seasonings. Bring to a boil. Reduce heat; simmer, uncovered, for 10 minutes to allow the flavors to blend, stirring occasionally. Serve on buns.

Nutrition Info:
- Info251 cal., 6g fat (2g sat. fat), 39mg chol., 629mg sod., 32g carb. (10g sugars, 2g fiber), 16g pro.

Spring Chicken & Pea Salad

Servings: 4
Cooking Time: 20 Minutes
Ingredients:
- 1 cup fresh peas
- 2 cups torn curly or Belgian endive
- 2 cups torn radicchio
- 2 cups chopped rotisserie chicken
- 1/2 cup sliced radishes
- 2 tablespoons chopped red onion
- 2 tablespoons fresh mint leaves, torn
- DRESSING
- 2 tablespoons olive oil
- 1/4 teaspoon grated lemon peel
- 1 tablespoon lemon juice
- 1 tablespoon mint jelly
- 1 garlic clove, minced
- 1/4 teaspoon salt
- 1/4 teaspoon pepper
- Toasted pine nuts, optional

Directions:
1. In a large saucepan, bring 1/2 in. of water to a boil. Add peas; cover and cook 5-8 minutes or until tender.
2. Drain the peas and place in a large bowl. Add endive, radicchio, chicken, radishes, onion and mint. In a small saucepan, combine oil, lemon peel, juice, jelly, garlic, salt and pepper; cook and stir over medium-low heat 4-6 minutes or until jelly is melted. Drizzle over the salad; toss to coat. If desired, sprinkle with pine nuts.

Nutrition Info:
- Info250 cal., 12g fat (2g sat. fat), 62mg chol., 225mg sod., 12g carb. (6g sugars, 3g fiber), 23g pro.

Bacon & Swiss Chicken Sandwiches

Servings: 4
Cooking Time: 25 Minutes
Ingredients:
- 1/4 cup reduced-fat mayonnaise
- 1 tablespoon Dijon mustard
- 1 tablespoon honey
- 4 boneless skinless chicken breast halves (4 ounces each)
- 1/2 teaspoon Montreal steak seasoning
- 4 slices Swiss cheese
- 4 whole wheat hamburger buns, split
- 2 bacon strips, cooked and crumbled
- Lettuce leaves and tomato slices, optional

Directions:
1. In a small bowl, mix mayonnaise, mustard and honey. Pound chicken with a meat mallet to 1/2-in. thickness. Sprinkle chicken with steak seasoning. Grill chicken, covered, over medium heat or broil 4 in. from heat 4-6 minutes on each side or until a thermometer reads 165°. Top with cheese during the last 1 minute of cooking.
2. Grill buns over medium heat, cut side down, for 30-60 seconds or until toasted. Serve chicken on buns with bacon, mayonnaise mixture and, if desired, lettuce and tomato.

Nutrition Info:
- Info410 cal., 17g fat (6g sat. fat), 91mg chol., 667mg sod., 29g carb. (9g sugars, 3g fiber), 34g pro.

Lemon Chicken With Orzo

Servings: 4
Cooking Time: 20 Minutes

Ingredients:

- 1/3 cup all-purpose flour
- 1 teaspoon garlic powder
- 1 pound boneless skinless chicken breasts
- 3/4 teaspoon salt, divided
- 1/2 teaspoon pepper
- 2 tablespoons olive oil
- 1 can (14 1/2 ounces) reduced-sodium chicken broth
- 1 1/4 cups uncooked whole wheat orzo pasta
- 2 cups chopped fresh spinach
- 1 cup grape tomatoes, halved
- 3 tablespoons lemon juice
- 2 tablespoons minced fresh basil
- Lemon wedges, optional

Directions:

1. In a shallow bowl, mix flour and garlic powder. Cut chicken into 1 1/2-in. pieces; pound each with a meat mallet to 1/4-in. thickness. Sprinkle with 1/2 teaspoon salt and pepper. Dip both sides of chicken in flour mixture to coat lightly; shake off any excess.
2. In a large skillet, heat the oil over medium heat. Add chicken; cook for 3-4 minutes on each side or until golden brown and chicken is no longer pink. Remove chicken from pan; keep warm. Wipe skillet clean.
3. In same pan, bring broth to a boil; stir in the orzo. Return to a boil. Reduce heat; simmer, covered, 8-10 minutes or until tender. Stir in the spinach, tomatoes, lemon juice, basil and remaining salt; remove from the heat. Return chicken to the pan. If desired, serve with lemon wedges.

Nutrition Info:

- Info399 cal., 11g fat (2g sat. fat), 63mg chol., 807mg sod., 43g carb. (2g sugars, 9g fiber), 32g pro.

Turkey Shepherd's Pie

Servings: 6
Cooking Time: 22 Minutes.

Ingredients:

- 3 tablespoons extra-virgin olive oil
- 1 large head cauliflower (3 pounds), cored and cut into ½-inch pieces
- ½ cup plus 2 tablespoons water
- Salt and pepper
- 1 large egg, lightly beaten
- 3 tablespoons minced fresh chives
- 1 pound ground turkey
- ¼ teaspoon baking soda
- 8 ounces cremini mushrooms, trimmed and chopped
- 1 onion, chopped
- 1 tablespoon no-salt-added tomato paste
- 2 garlic cloves, minced
- ¾ cup unsalted chicken broth
- 2 carrots, peeled and chopped
- 2 sprigs fresh thyme
- 1 tablespoon Worcestershire sauce
- 1 tablespoon cornstarch

Directions:

1. Heat 2 tablespoons oil in Dutch oven over medium-low heat until shimmering. Add cauliflower and cook, stirring occasionally, until softened and beginning to brown, 10 to 12 minutes. Stir in ½ cup water and ½ teaspoon salt, cover, and cook until cauliflower falls apart easily when poked with fork, about 10 minutes.
2. Transfer cauliflower and any remaining liquid to food processor and let cool for 5 minutes. Process until smooth, about 45 seconds, scraping down sides of bowl as needed. Transfer to large bowl and stir in egg and chives; set aside.
3. Meanwhile, toss turkey, 1 tablespoon water, baking soda, ¼ teaspoon salt, and ¼ teaspoon pepper in bowl until thoroughly combined. Set aside for 20 minutes.
4. Heat remaining 1 tablespoon oil in broiler-safe 10-inch skillet over medium heat until shimmering. Add mushrooms and onion and cook until liquid has evaporated and fond begins to form on bottom of skillet, 10 to 12 minutes. Stir in tomato paste and garlic and cook until bottom of skillet is dark brown, about 2 minutes.
5. Stir in broth, scraping up any browned bits. Stir in carrots, thyme sprigs, and Worcestershire, bring to simmer, and reduce heat to medium-low. Pinch off turkey in ½-inch pieces, add to skillet, and bring to gentle simmer. Cover and cook until turkey is cooked through, 8 to 10 minutes, stirring and breaking up meat into small pieces halfway through cooking.
6. Whisk cornstarch and remaining 1 tablespoon water together, then stir mixture into filling and continue to simmer until thickened, about 1 minute. Discard thyme sprigs and season with pepper to taste.
7. Adjust oven rack 5 inches from broiler element and heat broiler. Transfer cauliflower mixture to 1-gallon zipper-lock bag. Using scissors, snip 1 inch off filled corner. Squeezing bag, pipe mixture in even layer over filling, making sure to cover entire surface. Smooth mixture with back of spoon, then use tines of fork to make ridges over surface. Place skillet on aluminum foil-lined rimmed baking sheet and broil until topping is golden brown and crusty and filling is bubbly, 10 to 15 minutes. Let cool for 10 minutes before serving.

Nutrition Info:

- Info220 cal., 9g fat (2g sag. fat), 60mg chol, 490mg sod., 13g carb (5g sugars, 3g fiber), 23g pro.

Fish & Seafood Recipes

Shrimp-slaw Pitas

Servings: 6
Cooking Time: 5 Minutes
Ingredients:
- 1 1/2 pounds uncooked shrimp (31-40 per pound), peeled, deveined and coarsely chopped
- 1 tablespoon olive oil
- 1 teaspoon paprika
- SLAW
- 1/3 cup reduced-fat plain Greek yogurt
- 1/3 cup peach salsa or salsa of your choice
- 1 tablespoon honey
- 1/2 teaspoon salt
- 1/2 teaspoon pepper
- 1 package (12 ounces) broccoli coleslaw mix
- 2 cups fresh baby spinach
- 1/4 cup shredded carrots
- 1/4 cup frozen shelled edamame, thawed
- 12 whole wheat pita pocket halves

Directions:
1. Preheat broiler. In a small bowl, toss shrimp with oil and paprika. Transfer to a foil-lined 15x10x1-in. baking pan. Broil 4-5 in. from heat 3-4 minutes or until shrimp turn pink, stirring once.
2. In a small bowl, whisk yogurt, salsa, honey, salt and pepper. Add coleslaw mix, spinach, carrots, edamame and shrimp; toss to coat.
3. Place pita pockets on a baking sheet. Broil 4-5 in. from heat about 1-2 minutes on each side or until lightly toasted. Fill each pita half with 1/2 cup shrimp mixture.

Nutrition Info:
- Info322 cal., 6g fat (1g sat. fat), 139mg chol., 641mg sod., 41g carb. (7g sugars, 7g fiber), 28g pro.

Garlic-herb Salmon Sliders

Servings: 4
Cooking Time: 10 Minutes
Ingredients:
- 1/3 cup panko (Japanese) bread crumbs
- 4 teaspoons finely chopped shallot
- 2 teaspoons snipped fresh dill
- 1 tablespoon prepared horseradish
- 1 large egg, beaten
- 1/4 teaspoon salt
- 1/8 teaspoon pepper
- 1 pound salmon fillet, skin removed, cut into 1-inch cubes
- 8 whole wheat dinner rolls, split and toasted
- 1/4 cup reduced-fat garlic-herb spreadable cheese
- 8 small lettuce leaves

Directions:
1. In a large bowl, combine the first seven ingredients. Place salmon in food processor; pulse until coarsely chopped and add to bread crumb mixture. Mix lightly but thoroughly. Shape into eight 1/2-in.-thick patties.
2. On a lightly greased grill rack, grill burgers, covered, over medium heat or broil 4 in. from heat 3-4 minutes on each side or until a thermometer reads 160°. Serve on rolls with spreadable cheese and lettuce.

Nutrition Info:
- Info442 cal., 17g fat (5g sat. fat), 119mg chol., 676mg sod., 42g carb. (7g sugars, 6g fiber), 30g pro.

Poached Snapper With Sherry-tomato Vinaigrette

Servings: 4
Cooking Time: 30 Minutes

Ingredients:

- 4 (6-ounce) skinless red snapper fillets, 1 inch thick
- Salt and pepper
- ½ cup extra-virgin olive oil
- ½ onion, peeled
- 6 ounces cherry tomatoes (2 ounces cut into ⅛-inch-thick rounds)
- ½ small shallot, peeled
- 4 teaspoons sherry vinegar
- 1 tablespoon minced fresh parsley

Directions:

1. Adjust oven rack to middle position and heat oven to 250 degrees. Pat snapper dry with paper towels and sprinkle with ¼ teaspoon salt. Let sit at room temperature for 20 minutes.
2. Heat oil in 10-inch ovensafe nonstick skillet over medium heat until registers 180 degrees. Off heat, place onion half in center of skillet. Arrange fillets skinned side up around onion (oil should come roughly halfway up fillets) and spoon some oil over each fillet. Cover, transfer skillet to oven, and cook for 15 minutes.
3. Remove skillet from oven (skillet handle will be hot), then carefully flip fillets using 2 spatulas. Cover and continue to bake snapper until it registers 130 to 135 degrees, 9 to 14 minutes. Carefully transfer snapper to serving platter, reserving ¼ cup oil, and tent loosely with aluminum foil.
4. Process reserved ¼ cup fish cooking oil, whole tomatoes, shallot, vinegar, ⅛ teaspoon salt, and ½ teaspoon pepper in blender until smooth, about 2 minutes, scraping down sides of bowl as needed. Add any accumulated fish juices and blend for 10 seconds. Strain sauce through fine-mesh strainer into bowl; discard solids. To serve, spoon vinaigrette around fish. Garnish each fillet with parsley and tomato rounds. Serve.

Nutrition Info:

- Info310 cal., 16g fat (2g sag. fat), 65mg chol, 330mg sod., 2g carb (1g sugars, 1g fiber), 35g pro.

Shrimp And Sausage Rice

Servings: 4
Cooking Time: 23 Minutes

Ingredients:

- 4 ounces reduced-fat pork breakfast sausage
- 16 ounces frozen pepper stir-fry, thawed
- 1 1/4 cups water
- 3/4 cup instant brown rice
- 12 ounces peeled raw shrimp, rinsed and patted dry
- 1/4 teaspoon salt
- 1/4 teaspoon black pepper

Directions:

1. Place a large nonstick skillet over medium-high heat until hot. Coat the skillet with nonstick cooking spray, add the sausage, and cook until browned, breaking up large pieces while cooking. Set the sausage aside to drain on paper towels.
2. Recoat the skillet with nonstick cooking spray, add the pepper stir-fry mixture, increase the heat to high, and cook 3 minutes or until most of the liquid has evaporated.
3. Add the water and bring to a boil. Reduce the heat, cover tightly, and simmer 10 minutes or until vegetables are tender. Add the rice and shrimp, cover, and cook 5 minutes.
4. Remove from the heat and stir in the sausage, salt, and pepper. Cover tightly and let stand 5 minutes or until the liquid is absorbed.

Nutrition Info:

- Info280 cal., 6g fat (1g sag. fat), 115mg chol, 370mg sod., 35g carb (3g sugars, 3g fiber), 21g pro.

Lemon-pepper Tilapia With Mushrooms

Servings: 4
Cooking Time: 25 Minutes

Ingredients:
- 2 tablespoons butter
- 1/2 pound sliced fresh mushrooms
- 3/4 teaspoon lemon-pepper seasoning, divided
- 3 garlic cloves, minced
- 4 tilapia fillets (6 ounces each)
- 1/4 teaspoon paprika
- 1/8 teaspoon cayenne pepper
- 1 medium tomato, chopped
- 3 green onions, thinly sliced

Directions:
1. In a 12-in. skillet, heat butter over medium heat. Add mushrooms and 1/4 teaspoon lemon pepper; cook and stir 3-5 minutes or until tender. Add garlic; cook 30 seconds longer.
2. Place the fillets over mushrooms; sprinkle them with paprika, cayenne and remaining lemon pepper. Cook, covered, 5-7 minutes or until fish just begins to flake easily with a fork. Top with tomato and green onions.

Nutrition Info:
- Info216 cal., 8g fat (4g sat. fat), 98mg chol., 173mg sod., 5g carb. (2g sugars, 1g fiber), 34g pro.

Tomato-poached Halibut

Servings: 4
Cooking Time: 30 Minutes

Ingredients:
- 1 tablespoon olive oil
- 2 poblano peppers, finely chopped
- 1 small onion, finely chopped
- 1 can (14 1/2 ounces) fire-roasted diced tomatoes, undrained
- 1 can (14 1/2 ounces) no-salt-added diced tomatoes, undrained
- 1/4 cup chopped pitted green olives
- 3 garlic cloves, minced
- 1/4 teaspoon pepper
- 1/8 teaspoon salt
- 4 halibut fillets (4 ounces each)
- 1/3 cup chopped fresh cilantro
- 4 lemon wedges
- Crusty whole grain bread, optional

Directions:
1. In a large nonstick skillet, heat oil over medium-high heat. Add poblano peppers and onion; cook and stir about 4-6 minutes or until tender.
2. Stir in tomatoes, olives, garlic, pepper and salt. Bring to a boil. Adjust heat to maintain a gentle simmer. Add fillets. Cook, covered, 8-10 minutes or until fish just begins to flake easily with a fork. Sprinkle with cilantro. Serve with lemon wedges and, if desired, bread.

Nutrition Info:
- Info224 cal., 7g fat (1g sat. fat), 56mg chol., 651mg sod., 17g carb. (8g sugars, 4g fiber), 24g pro.

Salmon Cakes With Lemon-herb Sauce

Servings:4
Cooking Time:12 Minutes
Ingredients:

- ¼ cup low-fat plain yogurt
- 3 tablespoons minced fresh parsley
- 2 tablespoons mayonnaise
- 2 teaspoons lemon juice, plus lemon wedges for serving
- 1 scallion, minced
- Salt and pepper
- 1 shallot, minced
- 1 tablespoon Dijon mustard
- 2 teaspoons capers, rinsed and minced
- 1 (1¼-ounce) slice hearty 100 percent whole-wheat sandwich bread, crust removed, torn into 1-inch pieces
- 1 pound skinless salmon fillet, cut into 1-inch pieces
- 2 teaspoons extra-virgin olive oil

Directions:

1. Combine 2 tablespoons yogurt, 1 tablespoon parsley, mayonnaise, lemon juice, scallion, and pinch pepper in small bowl. Cover and refrigerate until ready to serve. Whisk shallot, remaining 2 tablespoons yogurt, remaining 2 tablespoons parsley, mustard, capers, ⅛ teaspoon salt, and ⅛ teaspoon pepper together in large bowl.
2. Pulse bread in food processor to coarse crumbs, about 4 pulses, then transfer to bowl with shallot mixture. Working in 2 batches, pulse salmon in now-empty food processor until coarsely ground, about 4 pulses; transfer to bowl with bread crumbs and gently toss until well combined. Pat salmon mixture into four ¾-inch-thick cakes, about 4 inches in diameter.
3. Heat oil in 12-inch nonstick skillet over medium heat until shimmering. Gently add cakes to skillet and cook until browned and centers are still translucent when checked with tip of paring knife and register 125 degrees (for medium-rare), 3 to 5 minutes per side. Serve with sauce and lemon wedges.

Nutrition Info:

- Info340 cal., 23g fat (4g sag. fat), 65mg chol, 350mg sod., 4g carb (2g sugars, 1g fiber), 25g pro.

Black Rice Bowls With Salmon

Servings:4
Cooking Time:40 Minutes
Ingredients:

- ¾ cup black rice
- Salt and pepper
- ¼ cup unseasoned rice vinegar
- ¼ cup mirin
- 1 tablespoon white miso
- 1 teaspoon grated fresh ginger
- ½ teaspoon grated lime zest plus 2 tablespoons juice
- 1 (1½-pound) skin-on salmon fillet, 1 inch thick
- 1 teaspoon extra-virgin olive oil
- 4 radishes, trimmed, halved, and sliced thin
- 1 cucumber, halved lengthwise, seeded, and sliced thin
- ½ avocado, sliced thin
- 2 scallions, sliced thin

Directions:

1. Bring 2 quarts water to boil in large saucepan over medium-high heat. Add rice and ½ teaspoon salt and cook until rice is tender, 20 to 25 minutes. Drain rice and transfer to large bowl.
2. Whisk vinegar, mirin, miso, ginger, lime zest and juice, ⅛ teaspoon salt, and ⅛ teaspoon pepper in small bowl until miso is fully incorporated. Measure out ¼ cup vinegar mixture and drizzle over rice. Let rice cool to room temperature, tossing occasionally, about 20 minutes. Set remaining dressing aside for serving.
3. While rice is cooking, adjust oven rack to lowest position, place aluminum foil–lined rimmed baking sheet on rack, and heat oven to 500 degrees. Cut salmon crosswise into 4 fillets. Pat salmon dry with paper towels, rub with oil, and sprinkle with ¼ teaspoon salt and ⅛ teaspoon pepper.
4. Once oven reaches 500 degrees, reduce oven temperature to 275 degrees. Remove sheet from oven and carefully place salmon skin-side down on hot sheet. Roast until centers are still translucent when checked with tip of paring knife and thickest part registers 125 degrees (for medium-rare), 4 to 6 minutes.
5. Flake salmon into large 3-inch pieces. Portion rice into 4 individual serving bowls and top with salmon, radishes, cucumber, and avocado. Sprinkle with scallions and drizzle with reserved dressing. Serve.

Nutrition Info:

- Info580 cal., 29g fat (6g sag. fat), 95mg chol, 490mg sod., 37g carb (7g sugars, 5g fiber), 39g pro.

Shrimp Piccata

Servings: 4
Cooking Time: 25 Minutes
Ingredients:
- 1/2 pound uncooked angel hair pasta
- 2 shallots, finely chopped
- 2 garlic cloves, minced
- 2 tablespoons olive oil
- 1 pound uncooked large shrimp, peeled and deveined
- 1 teaspoon dried oregano
- 1/8 teaspoon salt
- 1 cup chicken broth
- 1 cup white wine or additional chicken broth
- 4 teaspoons cornstarch
- 1/3 cup lemon juice
- 1/4 cup capers, drained
- 3 tablespoons minced fresh parsley

Directions:
1. Cook angel hair pasta according to package directions.
2. Meanwhile, in a large skillet, saute shallots and garlic in oil for 1 minute. Add the shrimp, oregano and salt; cook and stir until shrimp turn pink. In small bowl, combine the broth, wine and cornstarch; gradually stir into pan. Bring to a boil; cook and stir for 2 minutes or until thickened. Remove from the heat.
3. Drain pasta. Add the pasta, lemon juice, capers and parsley to the skillet; toss to coat.

Nutrition Info:
- Info295 cal., 9g fat (1g sat. fat), 139mg chol., 715mg sod., 27g carb. (2g sugars, 2g fiber), 22g pro.

Pan-seared Sesame-crusted Tuna Steaks

Servings: 4
Cooking Time: 8 Minutes
Ingredients:
- ¾ cup sesame seeds
- 4 (6-ounce) skinless tuna steaks, 1 inch thick
- 2 tablespoons canola oil
- ¼ teaspoon salt
- ⅛ teaspoon pepper

Directions:
1. Spread sesame seeds in shallow baking dish. Pat tuna steaks dry with paper towels, rub steaks all over with 1 tablespoon oil, then sprinkle with salt and pepper. Press both sides of each steak in sesame seeds to coat.
2. Heat remaining 1 tablespoon oil in 12-inch nonstick skillet over medium-high heat until just smoking. Place steaks in skillet and cook until seeds are golden and tuna is translucent red at center when checked with tip of paring knife and registers 110 degrees (for rare), 1 to 2 minutes per side. Transfer tuna to cutting board and slice ½ inch thick. Serve.

Nutrition Info:
- Info330 cal., 15g fat (1g sag. fat), 65mg chol, 250mg sod., 2g carb (0g sugars, 1g fiber), 45g pro.

Two-sauce Cajun Fish

Servings: 4
Cooking Time: 12–15 Minutes
Ingredients:
- 4 (4-ounce) tilapia filets (or any mild, lean white fish filets), rinsed and patted dry
- 1/2 teaspoon seafood seasoning
- 1 (14.5-ounce) can stewed tomatoes with Cajun seasonings, well drained
- 2 tablespoons no-trans-fat margarine (35% vegetable oil)

Directions:
1. Preheat the oven to 400°F.
2. Coat a broiler rack and pan with nonstick cooking spray, arrange the fish filets on the rack about 2 inches apart, and sprinkle them evenly with the seafood seasoning.
3. Place the tomatoes in a blender and puree until just smooth. Set aside 1/4 cup of the mixture in a small glass bowl.
4. Spoon the remaining tomatoes evenly over the top of each filet and bake 12–15 minutes or until the filets are opaque in the center.
5. Meanwhile, add the margarine to the reserved 1/4 cup tomato mixture and microwave on HIGH 20 seconds or until the mixture is just melted. Stir to blend well.
6. Place the filets on a serving platter, spoon the tomato-margarine mixture over the center of each filet, and sprinkle each lightly with chopped fresh parsley, if desired.

Nutrition Info:
- Info150 cal., 5g fat (1g sag. fat), 50mg chol, 250mg sod., 4g carb (3g sugars, 1g fiber), 23g pro.

Creamy Dill Sauce

Servings: 1
Cooking Time: 30 Minutes
Ingredients:
- This creamy sauce goes especially well with salmon.
- ¼ cup mayonnaise
- 2 tablespoons low-fat sour cream
- 1 small shallot, minced
- 1 tablespoon lemon juice
- 1 tablespoon minced fresh dill
- Water
- Pepper

Directions:
1. Combine mayonnaise, sour cream, shallot, lemon juice, and dill in bowl. Add water as needed to thin sauce consistency and season with pepper to taste. Cover and refrigerate for 30 minutes before serving. (Sauce can be refrigerated for up to 24 hours.)

Nutrition Info:
- Info100 cal., 11g fat (2g sag. fat), 5mg chol, 95mg sod., 1g carb (1g sugars, 0g fiber), 1g pro.

Cod In Coconut Broth With Lemon Grass And Ginger

Servings:4
Cooking Time:25 Minutes

Ingredients:
- 1 tablespoon canola oil
- 1 leek, white and light green parts only, halved lengthwise, sliced thin, and washed thoroughly
- 4 garlic cloves, minced
- 1 tablespoon grated fresh ginger
- 1 cup water
- 2 carrots, peeled and cut into 2-inch-long matchsticks
- 1 (10-inch) stalk lemon grass, trimmed to bottom 6 inches and bruised with back of knife
- 4 (6-ounce) skinless cod fillets, 1 to 1½ inches thick
- Salt and pepper
- ⅓ cup canned light coconut milk
- 1 tablespoon lime juice, plus lime wedges for serving
- 1 teaspoon fish sauce
- 2 tablespoons chopped dry-roasted peanuts
- 2 tablespoons fresh cilantro leaves
- 1 serrano chile, stemmed and sliced thin

Directions:
1. Heat oil in 12-inch nonstick skillet over medium heat until shimmering. Add leek and cook, stirring occasionally, until lightly browned, 4 to 6 minutes. Stir in garlic and ginger and cook until fragrant, about 30 seconds.
2. Stir in water, carrots, and lemon grass and bring to simmer. Pat cod dry with paper towels and sprinkle with ⅛ teaspoon salt and ⅛ teaspoon pepper. Nestle fish into skillet and bring to simmer. Reduce heat to low, cover, and cook until cod flakes apart when gently prodded with paring knife and registers 140 degrees, 8 to 12 minutes.
3. Carefully transfer fish to individual shallow serving bowls. Discard lemon grass. Using slotted spoon, divide leeks and carrots evenly among bowls. Off heat, whisk coconut milk, lime juice, and fish sauce into broth and season with pepper to taste. Ladle broth over fish. Sprinkle with peanuts, cilantro, and chile. Serve with lime wedges.

Nutrition Info:
- Info250 cal., 8g fat (2g sag. fat), 75mg chol, 290mg sod., 10g carb (3g sugars, 2g fiber), 33g pro.

Fantastic Fish Tacos

Servings:4
Cooking Time: 30 Minutes

Ingredients:
- 1/2 cup fat-free mayonnaise
- 1 tablespoon lime juice
- 2 teaspoons fat-free milk
- 1 large egg
- 1 teaspoon water
- 1/3 cup dry bread crumbs
- 2 tablespoons salt-free lemon-pepper seasoning
- 1 pound mahi mahi or cod fillets, cut into 1-inch strips
- 4 corn tortillas (6 inches), warmed
- TOPPINGS
- 1 cup coleslaw mix
- 2 medium tomatoes, chopped
- 1 cup shredded reduced-fat Mexican cheese blend
- 1 tablespoon minced fresh cilantro

Directions:
1. For the sauce, in a small bowl, mix the mayonnaise, lime juice and milk; refrigerate until serving.
2. In a shallow bowl, whisk together egg and water. In another bowl, toss bread crumbs with lemon pepper. Dip fish in egg mixture, then in crumb mixture, patting to help coating adhere.
3. Place a large nonstick skillet coated with cooking spray over medium-high heat. Add fish; cook 2-4 minutes per side or until golden brown and fish just begins to flake easily with a fork. Serve in tortillas with toppings and sauce.

Nutrition Info:
- Info321 cal., 10g fat (5g sat. fat), 148mg chol., 632mg sod., 29g carb. (5g sugars, 4g fiber), 34g pro.

Vegetables, Fruit And Side Dishes Recipes

Roasted Beans And Green Onions

Servings: 4
Cooking Time: 11 Minutes
Ingredients:
- 8 ounces green string beans, trimmed
- 4 whole green onions, trimmed and cut in fourths (about 3-inch pieces)
- 1 1/2 teaspoons extra virgin olive oil
- 1/4 teaspoon salt

Directions:
1. Preheat the oven to 425°F.
2. Line a baking sheet with foil and coat the foil with nonstick cooking spray.
3. Toss the beans, onions, and oil together in a medium bowl. Arrange them in a thin layer on the baking sheet.
4. Bake for 8 minutes and stir gently, using two utensils as you would for a stir-fry. Bake another 3–4 minutes or until the beans begin to brown on the edges and are tender-crisp.
5. Remove the pan from the oven and sprinkle the beans with salt.

Nutrition Info:
- Info35 cal., 2g fat (0g sag. fat), 0mg chol, 150mg sod., 5g carb (1g sugars, 2g fiber), 1g pro.

Orzo With Peppers & Spinach

Servings: 6
Cooking Time: 30 Minutes
Ingredients:
- 1 cup uncooked orzo pasta (about 8 ounces)
- 1 tablespoon olive oil
- 1 medium sweet orange pepper, chopped
- 1 medium sweet red pepper, chopped
- 1 medium sweet yellow pepper, chopped
- 1 cup sliced fresh mushrooms
- 3 garlic cloves, minced
- 1/2 teaspoon Italian seasoning
- 1/4 teaspoon salt
- 1/4 teaspoon pepper
- 2 cups fresh baby spinach
- 1/2 cup grated Parmesan cheese

Directions:
1. Cook orzo according to package directions; drain.
2. Meanwhile, in large skillet, heat oil over medium-high heat; saute peppers and mushrooms until tender. Add garlic and seasonings; cook and stir 1 minute.
3. Stir in the spinach until wilted. Stir in orzo and cheese; heat through.

Nutrition Info:
- Info196 cal., 5g fat (1g sat. fat), 6mg chol., 232mg sod., 30g carb. (4g sugars, 2g fiber), 7g pro.

Sautéed Spinach With Yogurt And Dukkah

Servings: 4
Cooking Time: 14 Minutes
Ingredients:
- ½ cup plain low-fat yogurt
- 1½ teaspoons grated lemon zest plus 1 teaspoon juice
- 3 tablespoons extra-virgin olive oil
- 20 ounces curly-leaf spinach, stemmed
- 2 garlic cloves, minced
- Salt and pepper
- ¼ cup dukkah

Directions:
1. Combine yogurt and lemon zest and juice in bowl; set aside for serving. Heat 1 tablespoon oil in Dutch oven over high heat until shimmering. Add spinach, 1 handful at a time, stirring and tossing each handful to wilt slightly before adding more. Cook spinach, stirring constantly, until uniformly wilted, about 1 minute. Transfer spinach to colander and squeeze between tongs to release excess liquid.
2. Wipe pot dry with paper towels. Add remaining 2 tablespoons oil and garlic to now-empty pot and cook over medium heat until fragrant, about 30 seconds. Add spinach and ⅛ teaspoon salt and toss to coat, gently separating leaves to evenly coat with garlic oil. Off heat, season with pepper to taste. Transfer spinach to serving platter, drizzle with yogurt sauce, and sprinkle with dukkah. Serve.

Nutrition Info:
- Info180 cal., 13g fat (2g sag. fat), 0mg chol, 320mg sod., 10g carb (2g sugars, 4g fiber), 6g pro.

Basil Grilled Corn On The Cob

Servings: 4
Cooking Time: 20 Minutes
Ingredients:
- 4 medium ears sweet corn
- 4 teaspoons butter, melted
- 3/4 teaspoon salt
- 1/4 teaspoon pepper
- 16 fresh basil leaves
- 1/2 medium lemon
- 2 teaspoons minced fresh cilantro
- Additional butter, optional

Directions:
1. Place corn in a 6-qt. stockpot; cover with cold water. Soak 20 minutes; drain. Carefully peel back corn husks to within 1 in. of bottoms; remove silk. Brush butter over corn; sprinkle with salt and pepper. Press four basil leaves onto each cob. Rewrap corn in husks; secure with kitchen string.
2. Grill corn, covered, over medium heat 20-25 minutes or until tender, turning often. Cut string and peel back husks; discard basil leaves. Squeeze lemon juice over corn; sprinkle with cilantro. If desired, spread the corn with additional butter.

Nutrition Info:
- Info125 cal., 5g fat (3g sat. fat), 10mg chol., 489mg sod., 20g carb. (7g sugars, 2g fiber), 4g pro.

Broiled Eggplant With Basil

Servings: 6
Cooking Time: 9 Minutes
Ingredients:
- 1½ pounds eggplant, sliced into ¼-inch-thick rounds
- Kosher salt and pepper
- 3 tablespoons extra-virgin olive oil
- 2 tablespoons chopped fresh basil

Directions:
1. Spread eggplant on paper towel–lined baking sheet, sprinkle both sides with 1½ teaspoons salt, and let sit for 9 minutes.
2. Adjust oven rack 4 inches from broiler element and heat broiler. Thoroughly pat eggplant dry with paper towels, arrange on aluminum foil–lined rimmed baking sheet in single layer, and brush both sides with oil. Broil eggplant until mahogany brown and lightly charred, about 4 minutes per side. Transfer eggplant to serving platter, season with pepper to taste, and sprinkle with basil. Serve.

Nutrition Info:
- Info90 cal., 7g fat (1g sag. fat), 0mg chol, 140mg sod., 7g carb (4g sugars, 3g fiber), 1g pro.

Crunchy Pear And Cilantro Relish

Servings: 4
Cooking Time: 6 Minutes
Ingredients:
- 2 firm medium pears, peeled, cored, and finely chopped (about 1/4-inch cubes)
- 3/4 teaspoon lime zest
- 3 tablespoons lime juice
- 1 1/4 tablespoons sugar
- 3 tablespoons chopped cilantro or mint

Directions:
1. Place all ingredients in a bowl and toss well.
2. Serve immediately for peak flavor and texture.

Nutrition Info:
- Info50 cal., 0g fat (0g sag. fat), 0mg chol, 0mg sod., 14g carb (9g sugars, 3g fiber), 0g pro.

Roasted Root Vegetables With Lemon-caper Sauce

Servings:6
Cooking Time: 35 Minutes
Ingredients:
- 1 pound Brussels sprouts, trimmed and halved
- 1 pound red potatoes, unpeeled, cut into 1-inch pieces
- 8 shallots, peeled and halved
- 4 carrots, peeled and cut into 2-inch lengths, thick ends halved lengthwise
- 6 garlic cloves, peeled
- 3 tablespoons extra-virgin olive oil
- 2 teaspoons minced fresh thyme
- 1 teaspoon minced fresh rosemary
- Salt and pepper
- 2 tablespoons minced fresh parsley
- 1½ tablespoons capers, rinsed and minced
- 1 tablespoon lemon juice, plus extra for seasoning

Directions:
1. Adjust oven rack to middle position and heat oven to 450 degrees. Toss Brussels sprouts, potatoes, shallots, and carrots with garlic, 1 tablespoon oil, thyme, rosemary, ½ teaspoon salt, and ¼ teaspoon pepper.
2. Spread vegetables into single layer on rimmed baking sheet, arranging Brussels sprouts cut side down in center of sheet. Roast until vegetables are tender and golden brown, 30 to 35 minutes, rotating sheet halfway through roasting.
3. Whisk parsley, capers, lemon juice, and remaining 2 tablespoons oil together in large bowl. Add roasted vegetables and toss to combine. Season with pepper and extra lemon juice to taste. Serve.

Nutrition Info:
- Info200 cal., 8g fat (1g sag. fat), 0mg chol, 310mg sod., 31g carb (8g sugars, 7g fiber), 5g pro.

Sautéed Swiss Chard With Garlic

Servings:6
Cooking Time:8 Minutes
Ingredients:
- 2 tablespoons extra-virgin olive oil
- 3 garlic cloves, sliced thin
- 1½ pounds Swiss chard, stems sliced ¼ inch thick on bias, leaves sliced into ½-inch-wide strips
- 2 teaspoons lemon juice
- Pepper

Directions:
1. Heat oil in 12-inch nonstick skillet over medium-high heat until just shimmering. Add garlic and cook, stirring constantly, until lightly browned, 30 to 60 seconds. Add chard stems and cook, stirring occasionally, until spotty brown and crisp-tender, about 6 minutes.
2. Add two-thirds of chard leaves and cook, tossing with tongs, until just starting to wilt, 30 to 60 seconds. Add remaining chard leaves and continue to cook, stirring frequently, until leaves are tender, about 3 minutes. Off heat, stir in lemon juice and season with pepper to taste. Serve.

Nutrition Info:
- Info60 cal., 5g fat (0g sag. fat), 0mg chol, 220mg sod., 5g carb (1g sugars, 2g fiber), 2g pro.

Balsamic Zucchini Saute

Servings: 4
Cooking Time: 20 Minutes
Ingredients:
- 1 tablespoon olive oil
- 3 medium zucchini, cut into thin slices
- 1/2 cup chopped sweet onion
- 1/2 teaspoon salt
- 1/2 teaspoon dried rosemary, crushed
- 1/4 teaspoon pepper
- 2 tablespoons balsamic vinegar
- 1/3 cup crumbled feta cheese

Directions:
1. In a large skillet, heat oil over medium-high heat; saute zucchini and onion until crisp-tender, 6-8 minutes. Stir in the seasonings. Add vinegar; cook and stir 2 minutes. Top with cheese.

Nutrition Info:
- Info94 cal., 5g fat (2g sat. fat), 5mg chol., 398mg sod., 9g carb. (6g sugars, 2g fiber), 4g pro.

Pesto Pasta & Potatoes

Servings: 12
Cooking Time: 30 Minutes
Ingredients:
- 1 1/2 pounds small red potatoes, halved
- 12 ounces uncooked whole grain spiral pasta
- 3 cups cut fresh or frozen green beans
- 1 jar (6 1/2 ounces) prepared pesto
- 1 cup grated Parmigiano-Reggiano cheese

Directions:
1. Place potatoes in a large saucepan; add water to cover. Bring to a boil. Reduce heat; cook, uncovered, until tender, 8-10 minutes. Drain; transfer to a large bowl.
2. Meanwhile, cook pasta according to package directions, adding green beans during the last 5 minutes of cooking. Drain, reserving 3/4 cup pasta water, and add to potatoes. Toss with the pesto, cheese blend and enough pasta water to moisten.

Nutrition Info:
- Info261 cal., 10g fat (3g sat. fat), 11mg chol., 233mg sod., 34g carb. (2g sugars, 5g fiber), 11g pro.

Tomato-onion Green Beans

Servings: 6
Cooking Time: 30 Minutes
Ingredients:
- 2 tablespoons olive oil
- 1 large onion, finely chopped
- 1 pound fresh green beans, trimmed
- 3 tablespoons tomato paste
- 1/2 teaspoon salt
- 2 tablespoons minced fresh parsley

Directions:
1. In a large skillet, heat the oil over medium-high heat. Add chopped onion; cook until tender and lightly browned, stirring occasionally.
2. Meanwhile, place green beans in a large saucepan; add water to cover. Bring to a boil. Cook, covered, for 5-7 minutes or until crisp-tender. Drain; add to onion. Stir in tomato paste and salt; heat through. Sprinkle with parsley.

Nutrition Info:
- Info81 cal., 5g fat (1g sat. fat), 0 chol., 208mg sod., 9g carb. (4g sugars, 3g fiber), 2g pro.

Marinated Eggplant With Capers And Mint

Servings: 6
Cooking Time: 40 Minutes
Ingredients:
- 1½ pounds Italian eggplant, sliced into 1-inch-thick rounds
- Kosher salt and pepper
- ¼ cup extra-virgin olive oil
- 4 teaspoons red wine vinegar
- 1 tablespoon capers, rinsed and minced
- 1 garlic clove, minced
- ½ teaspoon grated lemon zest
- ½ teaspoon minced fresh oregano
- 3 tablespoons minced fresh mint

Directions:
1. Spread eggplant on paper towel–lined baking sheet, sprinkle both sides with ½ teaspoon salt, and let sit for 30 minutes.
2. Adjust oven rack 4 inches from broiler element and heat broiler. Thoroughly pat eggplant dry with paper towels, arrange on aluminum foil–lined rimmed baking sheet in single layer, and lightly brush both sides with 1 tablespoon oil. Broil eggplant until mahogany brown and lightly charred, 6 to 8 minutes per side.
3. Whisk remaining 3 tablespoons oil, vinegar, capers, garlic, lemon zest, oregano, and ¼ teaspoon pepper together in large bowl. Add eggplant and mint and gently toss to combine. Let eggplant cool to room temperature, about 1 hour. Season with pepper to taste and serve.

Nutrition Info:
- Info120 cal., 10g fat (1g sag. fat), 0mg chol, 85mg sod., 7g carb (4g sugars, 3g fiber), 1g pro.

Sautéed Green Beans With Garlic And Herbs

Servings: 4
Cooking Time: 14 Minutes
Ingredients:
- 4 teaspoons extra-virgin olive oil
- 3 garlic cloves, minced
- 1 teaspoon minced fresh thyme
- 1 pound green beans, trimmed and cut into 2-inch lengths
- Salt and pepper
- 2 teaspoons lemon juice
- 1 tablespoon minced fresh parsley, basil, and/or mint

Directions:
1. Combine 1 tablespoon oil, garlic, and thyme in bowl. Heat remaining 1 teaspoon oil in 12-inch nonstick skillet over medium heat until just smoking. Add beans, ¼ teaspoon salt, and ⅛ teaspoon pepper and cook, stirring occasionally, until spotty brown, 4 to 6 minutes. Add ¼ cup water, cover, and cook until beans are bright green and still crisp, about 2 minutes.
2. Uncover, increase heat to high, and cook until water evaporates, 30 to 60 seconds. Add oil mixture and cook, stirring often, until beans are crisp-tender, lightly browned, and beginning to wrinkle, 1 to 3 minutes. Off heat, stir in lemon juice and parsley and season with pepper to taste. Serve.

Nutrition Info:
- Info80 cal., 5g fat (0g sag. fat), 0mg chol, 150mg sod., 8g carb (3g sugars, 3g fiber), 2g pro.

Saucy Eggplant And Capers

Servings: 4
Cooking Time: 21 Minutes
Ingredients:
- 10 ounces eggplant, diced (about 2 1/2 cups)
- 1 (14.5-ounce) can stewed tomatoes with Italian seasonings
- 2 tablespoons chopped fresh basil
- 2 teaspoons capers, drained
- 2 teaspoons extra virgin olive oil (optional)

Directions:
1. Bring the eggplant and tomatoes to boil in a large saucepan over high heat. Reduce the heat, cover tightly, and simmer 20 minutes or until the eggplant is very tender.
2. Remove the saucepan from the heat, stir in the basil, capers, and 2 teaspoons extra virgin olive oil (if desired), and let stand 3 minutes to develop flavors.

Nutrition Info:
- Info50 cal., 0g fat (0g sag. fat), 0mg chol, 250mg sod., 12g carb (7g sugars, 3g fiber), 2g pro.

Vegetarian Recipes

Chickpea Cakes With Cucumber-yogurt Sauce

Servings: 4
Cooking Time: 15 Minutes

Ingredients:
- CUCUMBER-YOGURT SAUCE
- 1 cucumber, peeled, halved lengthwise, seeded, and shredded
- Salt and pepper
- 1 cup 2 percent Greek yogurt
- 2 tablespoons extra-virgin olive oil
- 2 tablespoons minced fresh cilantro
- 1 garlic clove, minced
- CHICKPEA CAKES
- 2 (15-ounce) cans no-salt-added chickpeas, rinsed
- ½ cup 2 percent Greek yogurt
- 2 large eggs
- 5 tablespoons extra-virgin olive oil
- 1 teaspoon garam masala
- ¼ teaspoon salt
- ⅛ teaspoon cayenne pepper
- 1 cup 100 percent whole-wheat panko bread crumbs
- 5 scallions, sliced thin
- 3 tablespoons minced fresh cilantro
- 1 shallot, minced

Directions:
1. FOR THE CUCUMBER-YOGURT SAUCE Toss cucumber with ½ teaspoon salt in fine-mesh strainer and let drain for 15 minutes. Combine drained cucumber with yogurt, oil, cilantro, and garlic and season with pepper to taste. (Sauce can be refrigerated for up to 1 day.)
2. FOR THE CHICKPEA CAKES Line rimmed baking sheet with parchment paper. Pulse chickpeas in food processor to coarse puree with few large pieces remaining, about 8 pulses.
3. In medium bowl, whisk yogurt, eggs, 2 tablespoons oil, garam masala, salt, and cayenne together. Stir in chickpeas, panko, scallions, cilantro, and shallot until combined. Divide mixture into 8 equal portions, pack firmly into 1-inch-thick patties, and place on prepared sheet. Cover and refrigerate patties for at least 1 hour and up to 24 hours.
4. Heat 1½ tablespoons oil in 12-inch nonstick skillet over medium heat until shimmering. Gently lay 4 patties in skillet and cook until well browned on first side, 6 to 8 minutes. Gently flip patties and cook until golden brown on second side, 6 to 8 minutes. Transfer patties to serving platter and tent with aluminum foil. Return now-empty skillet to medium heat and repeat with remaining 1½ tablespoons oil and remaining patties. Serve with cucumber-yogurt sauce.

Nutrition Info:
- Info540 cal., 30g fat (5g sag. fat), 95mg chol, 410mg sod., 44g carb (7g sugars, 9g fiber), 22g pro.

Stewed Chickpeas With Eggplant And Tomatoes

Servings: 6
Cooking Time: 60 Minutes

Ingredients:

- ¼ cup extra-virgin olive oil
- 2 onions, chopped
- 1 green bell pepper, stemmed, seeded, and chopped fine
- Salt and pepper
- 3 garlic cloves, minced
- 1 tablespoon minced fresh oregano or 1 teaspoon dried
- 2 bay leaves
- 1 pound eggplant, cut into 1-inch pieces
- 1 (28-ounce) can no-salt-added whole peeled tomatoes, drained with juice reserved, chopped coarse
- 2 (15-ounce) cans no-salt-added chickpeas, drained with 1 cup liquid reserved

Directions:

1. Adjust oven rack to lower-middle position and heat oven to 400 degrees. Heat oil in Dutch oven over medium heat until shimmering. Add onions, bell pepper, ½ teaspoon salt, and ¼ teaspoon pepper and cook until softened, about 5 minutes. Stir in garlic, 1 teaspoon oregano, and bay leaves and cook until fragrant, about 30 seconds.
2. Stir in eggplant, tomatoes and reserved juice, and chickpeas and reserved liquid and bring to boil. Transfer pot to oven and cook, uncovered, until eggplant is very tender, 45 to 60 minutes, stirring twice during cooking.
3. Discard bay leaves. Stir in remaining 2 teaspoons oregano and season with pepper to taste. Serve.

Nutrition Info:

- Info270 cal., 10g fat (1g sag. fat), 0mg chol, 470mg sod., 34g carb (9g sugars, 9g fiber), 9g pro.

Mexican-style Spaghetti Squash Casserole

Servings: 4
Cooking Time: 45 Minutes

Ingredients:

- 1 (2½- to 3-pound) spaghetti squash, halved lengthwise and seeded
- 3 tablespoons extra-virgin olive oil
- Salt and pepper
- 2 garlic cloves, minced
- ½ teaspoon smoked paprika
- ½ teaspoon ground cumin
- 1 (15-ounce) can no-salt-added black beans, rinsed
- 1 cup frozen corn
- 6 ounces cherry tomatoes, quartered
- 6 scallions (4 minced, 2 sliced thin)
- 1 jalapeño chile, stemmed, seeded, and minced
- 1 avocado, halved, pitted, and cut into ½-inch pieces
- 2 ounces queso fresco, crumbled (½ cup)
- Lime wedges

Directions:

1. Adjust oven rack to middle position and heat oven to 375 degrees. Lightly spray 8-inch square baking dish with vegetable oil spray. Brush cut sides of squash with 1 tablespoon oil and sprinkle with ⅛ teaspoon salt and ¼ teaspoon pepper. Place squash cut side down in prepared dish (squash will not sit flat in dish) and roast until just tender, 40 to 45 minutes. Flip squash cut side up and let sit until cool enough to handle, about 20 minutes. Do not turn off oven.
2. Combine remaining 2 tablespoons oil, garlic, paprika, cumin, and ½ teaspoon salt in large bowl and microwave until fragrant, about 30 seconds. Stir in beans, corn, tomatoes, minced scallions, and jalapeño.
3. Using fork, scrape squash into strands in bowl with bean mixture. Stir to combine, then spread mixture evenly in now-empty dish and cover tightly with aluminum foil. Bake until heated through, 20 to 25 minutes. Sprinkle with avocado, queso fresco, and sliced scallions. Serve with lime wedges.

Nutrition Info:

- Info400 cal., 24g fat (4g sag. fat), 10mg chol, 520mg sod., 41g carb (9g sugars, 11g fiber), 11g pro.

Sweet Potato, Poblano, And Black Bean Tacos

Servings: 6
Cooking Time: 30 Minutes
Ingredients:
- ½ cup red wine vinegar
- ½ teaspoon red pepper flakes
- 1 red onion, halved and sliced thin
- 3 tablespoons extra-virgin olive oil
- 3 garlic cloves, minced
- 1½ teaspoons ground cumin
- 1½ teaspoons ground coriander
- 1 teaspoon minced fresh oregano or ¼ teaspoon dried
- Salt and pepper
- 1 pound sweet potatoes, peeled and cut into ½-inch pieces
- 4 poblano chiles, stemmed, seeded, and cut into ½-inch-wide strips
- 1 (15-ounce) can no-salt added black beans, rinsed
- ¼ cup chopped fresh cilantro
- 12 (6-inch) corn tortillas, warmed
- 1 avocado, halved, pitted, and cut into ½-inch pieces

Directions:
1. Adjust oven racks to upper-middle and lower-middle positions and heat oven to 450 degrees. Line 2 rimmed baking sheets with aluminum foil. Microwave vinegar and pepper flakes in medium bowl until steaming, about 2 minutes. Stir in onion and let sit until ready to serve.
2. Whisk oil, garlic, cumin, coriander, oregano, ½ teaspoon salt, and ½ teaspoon pepper together in large bowl. Add potatoes and poblanos to oil mixture and toss to coat.
3. Spread vegetable mixture in even layer in lined baking sheets. Roast vegetables until tender and golden brown, about 30 minutes, stirring vegetables and switching and rotating sheets halfway through baking.
4. Return vegetables to now-empty bowl, add black beans and cilantro, and gently toss to combine. Divide vegetables evenly among warm tortillas and top with avocado and pickled onions. Serve.

Nutrition Info:
- Info350 cal., 14g fat (2g sag. fat), 0mg chol, 250mg sod., 51g carb (7g sugars, 11g fiber), 8g pro.

Light Parmesan Pasta

Servings: 4
Cooking Time: 8 Minutes
Ingredients:
- 8 ounces uncooked whole-wheat no-yolk egg noodles
- 1/4–1/3 cup fat-free evaporated milk
- 6 tablespoons grated Parmesan cheese (divided use)
- 1 tablespoon no-trans-fat margarine (35% vegetable oil)
- 1/2 teaspoon salt
- 1/4 teaspoon black pepper

Directions:
1. Cook the pasta according to package directions, omitting any salt or fat.
2. Drain the pasta well and place it in a medium bowl. Add the remaining ingredients except 1 tablespoon Parmesan cheese. Toss to blend, then sprinkle with 1 tablespoon Parmesan on top.

Nutrition Info:
- Info230 cal., 4g fat (1g sag. fat), 5mg chol, 450mg sod., 44g carb (2g sugars, 6g fiber), 12g pro.

Stuffed Eggplant With Bulgur

Servings: 4
Cooking Time: 40 Minutes

Ingredients:

- 4 (10-ounce) Italian eggplants, halved lengthwise
- ¼ cup extra-virgin olive oil
- Salt and pepper
- ½ cup medium-grind bulgur, rinsed
- ¼ cup water
- 1 onion, chopped fine
- 3 garlic cloves, minced
- 2 teaspoons minced fresh oregano or ½ teaspoon dried
- ¼ teaspoon ground cinnamon
- ⅛ teaspoon cayenne pepper
- 1 pound plum tomatoes, cored, seeded, and chopped
- 2 ounces Pecorino Romano cheese, grated (1 cup)
- 2 tablespoons pine nuts, toasted
- ¼ teaspoon grated lemon zest plus 1 tablespoon juice
- 2 tablespoons minced fresh parsley
- Lemon wedges

Directions:

1. Adjust oven racks to upper-middle and lowest positions, place parchment paper–lined rimmed baking sheet on lowest rack, and heat oven to 400 degrees.
2. Score flesh of each eggplant half in 1-inch crosshatch pattern, about 1 inch deep. Brush scored sides of eggplant with 1 tablespoon oil and sprinkle with ⅛ teaspoon salt and ¼ teaspoon pepper. Lay eggplant cut side down on hot sheet and roast until flesh is tender, 40 to 50 minutes. Transfer eggplant cut side down to paper towel–lined baking sheet and let drain. Do not wash rimmed baking sheet.
3. Meanwhile, toss bulgur with water in bowl and let sit until grains are softened and liquid is fully absorbed, 20 to 40 minutes.
4. Heat 1 tablespoon oil in 12-inch skillet over medium heat until shimmering. Add onion and cook until softened, 5 minutes. Stir in garlic, oregano, cinnamon, cayenne, and ¼ teaspoon salt and cook until fragrant, about 30 seconds. Stir in bulgur, tomatoes, ¾ cup Pecorino, pine nuts, and lemon zest and juice and cook until heated through, about 1 minute. Season with pepper to taste.
5. Return eggplant cut side up to rimmed baking sheet. Using 2 forks, gently push eggplant flesh to sides to make room for filling. Mound bulgur mixture into eggplant halves and pack lightly with back of spoon. Sprinkle with remaining ¼ cup Pecorino. Bake on upper-middle rack until cheese is melted, 5 to 10 minutes. Drizzle with remaining 2 tablespoons oil, sprinkle with parsley, and serve with lemon wedges.

Nutrition Info:

- Info370 cal., 22g fat (5g sag. fat), 15mg chol, 320mg sod., 39g carb (14g sugars, 12g fiber), 11g pro.

Curried Tempeh With Cauliflower And Peas

Servings: 6
Cooking Time: 15 Minutes

Ingredients:
- 1 (14.5-ounce) no-salt-added can diced tomatoes
- ¼ cup canola oil
- 2 tablespoons curry powder
- 1½ teaspoons garam masala
- 2 onions, chopped fine
- Salt and pepper
- 3 garlic cloves, minced
- 1 tablespoon grated fresh ginger
- 1 serrano chile, stemmed, seeded, and minced
- 1 tablespoon no-salt-added tomato paste
- ½ head cauliflower (1 pound), cored and cut into 1-inch florets
- 8 ounces tempeh, cut into 1-inch pieces
- 1¼ cups water
- 1 cup frozen peas
- ¼ cup light coconut milk
- 2 tablespoons minced fresh cilantro
- Lime wedges

Directions:
1. Pulse diced tomatoes with their juice in food processor until nearly smooth, with some ¼-inch pieces visible, about 3 pulses.
2. Heat oil in Dutch oven over medium-high heat until shimmering. Add curry powder and garam masala and cook until fragrant, about 10 seconds. Add onions and ¼ teaspoon salt and cook, stirring occasionally, until softened and browned, about 10 minutes.
3. Reduce heat to medium. Stir in garlic, ginger, serrano, and tomato paste and cook until fragrant, about 30 seconds. Add cauliflower and tempeh and cook, stirring constantly, until florets are coated with spices, about 2 minutes.
4. Gradually stir in water, scraping up any browned bits. Stir in tomatoes and bring to simmer. Cover, reduce heat to low, and cook until vegetables are tender, 10 to 15 minutes.
5. Stir in peas, coconut milk, and ¾ teaspoon salt and cook until heated through, 1 to 2 minutes. Off heat, stir in cilantro and season with pepper to taste. Serve with lime wedges.

Nutrition Info:
- Info 240 cal., 15g fat (2g sag. fat), 0mg chol, 430mg sod., 19g carb (6g sugars, 6g fiber), 12g pro.

Cheesy Spinach-stuffed Shells

Servings: 12
Cooking Time: 45 Minutes

Ingredients:
- 1 package (12 ounces) jumbo pasta shells
- 1 tablespoon butter
- 1 cup sliced mushrooms
- 1 small onion, finely chopped
- 4 garlic cloves, minced
- 2 large eggs, lightly beaten
- 1 carton (15 ounces) part-skim ricotta cheese
- 1 package (10 ounces) frozen chopped spinach, thawed and squeezed dry
- 2 tablespoons minced fresh basil or 2 teaspoons dried basil
- 1/4 teaspoon pepper
- 1 can (4 1/4 ounces) chopped ripe olives
- 1 1/2 cups shredded Italian cheese blend, divided
- 1 1/2 cups shredded part-skim mozzarella cheese, divided
- 1 jar (24 ounces) marinara sauce
- Additional minced fresh basil, optional

Directions:
1. Preheat oven to 375°. Cook the pasta shells according to the package directions for al dente. Drain; rinse with cold water.
2. Meanwhile, in a small skillet, heat butter over medium-high heat. Add mushrooms and onion; cook and stir 4-6 minutes or until vegetables are tender. Add garlic; cook 1 minute longer. Remove from heat; cool slightly.
3. In a bowl, mix eggs, ricotta cheese, spinach, basil and pepper. Stir in olives, mushroom mixture and 3/4 cup each cheese blend and mozzarella cheese.
4. Spread 1 cup sauce into a 13x9-in. baking dish coated with cooking spray. Fill shells with cheese mixture; place in baking dish, overlapping ends slightly. Spoon remaining sauce over top.
5. Bake, covered, 40-45 minutes or until heated through. Uncover; sprinkle with remaining cheeses. Bake 5 minutes longer or until cheese is melted. Let stand 5 minutes before serving. If desired, sprinkle with additional basil.

Nutrition Info:
- Info 313 cal., 13g fat (7g sat. fat), 65mg chol., 642mg sod., 32g carb. (5g sugars, 3g fiber), 18g pro.

Vegan Black Bean Burgers

Servings: 6
Cooking Time: 15 Minutes

Ingredients:
- 2 (15-ounce) cans no-salt-added black beans, drained, with 6 tablespoons bean liquid reserved, and rinsed
- 2 tablespoons all-purpose flour
- 4 scallions, minced
- 3 tablespoons minced fresh cilantro
- 2 garlic cloves, minced
- 1 teaspoon ground cumin
- 1 teaspoon hot sauce (optional)
- ½ teaspoon ground coriander
- ½ teaspoon salt
- ¼ teaspoon pepper
- 1 ounce corn tortilla chips, crushed (½ cup)
- ¼ cup canola oil
- 6 100 percent whole-wheat burger buns, lightly toasted (optional)
- 2 avocados, halved, pitted, and sliced ¼ inch thick
- 1 head Bibb lettuce (8 ounces), leaves separated
- 2 tomatoes, cored and sliced ¼ inch thick

Directions:
1. Line rimmed baking sheet with triple layer of paper towels, spread beans over towels, and let sit for 15 minutes.
2. Whisk reserved bean liquid and flour in large bowl until well combined and smooth. Stir in scallions, cilantro, garlic, cumin, hot sauce, if using, coriander, salt, and pepper until well combined. Process tortilla chips in food processor until finely ground, about 30 seconds. Add black beans and pulse until beans are coarsely ground, about 5 pulses. Transfer bean mixture to bowl with flour mixture and mix until well combined.
3. Adjust oven rack to middle position and heat oven to 200 degrees. Divide mixture into 6 equal portions and pack firmly into 3½-inch-wide patties.
4. Heat 1 tablespoon oil in 10-inch nonstick skillet over medium heat until shimmering. Gently lay 3 patties in skillet and cook until crisp and well browned on first side, about 5 minutes. Gently flip patties, add 1 tablespoon oil, and cook until crisp and well browned on second side, 3 to 5 minutes.
5. Transfer burgers to wire rack set in rimmed baking sheet and place in oven to keep warm. Wipe out skillet with paper towels and repeat with remaining 2 tablespoons oil and remaining patties. Serve burgers on buns, if using, and top with avocado, lettuce, and tomatoes.

Nutrition Info:
- Info450 cal., 24g fat (2g sag. fat), 0mg chol, 460mg sod., 52g carb (6g sugars, 15g fiber), 13g pro.

Eggplant Involtini

Servings: 4
Cooking Time: 15 Minutes

Ingredients:

- 2 large eggplants (1½ pounds each), peeled and sliced lengthwise into ½-inch-thick planks (about 12 planks), end pieces trimmed to lie flat
- 6 tablespoons canola oil
- Salt and pepper
- 2 garlic cloves, minced
- ¼ teaspoon dried oregano
- Pinch red pepper flakes
- 1 (28-ounce) can no-salt-added whole peeled tomatoes, drained, juice reserved, and tomatoes chopped coarse
- 8 ounces (1 cup) whole-milk ricotta cheese
- 1 ounce Pecorino Romano cheese, grated (½ cup)
- ¼ cup plus 1 tablespoon chopped fresh basil
- 1 tablespoon lemon juice

Directions:

1. Adjust 1 oven rack to lower-middle position and second rack 8 inches from broiler element. Heat oven to 375 degrees. Line 2 rimmed baking sheets with parchment paper and spray generously with vegetable oil spray. Brush 1 side of eggplant slices with 2½ tablespoons oil, then season with ⅛ teaspoon salt and ¼ teaspoon pepper. Flip slices over and repeat on second side with another 2½ tablespoons oil, ⅛ teaspoon salt, and ¼ teaspoon pepper. Arrange eggplant slices in single layer on prepared sheets. Bake until tender and lightly browned, 30 to, switching and rotating sheets halfway through baking. Let eggplant cool for 5 minutes, then flip each slice over using thin spatula.
2. Heat remaining 1 tablespoon oil in 12-inch broiler-safe skillet over medium-low heat until shimmering. Add garlic, ⅛ teaspoon salt, oregano, and pepper flakes and cook, stirring occasionally, until fragrant, about 30 seconds. Stir in tomatoes and their juice, bring to simmer, and cook until thickened, about 15 minutes. Cover to keep warm.
3. Combine ricotta, ¼ cup Pecorino, ¼ cup basil, and lemon juice in bowl. With widest short side facing you, spoon about 1 tablespoon ricotta mixture over bottom third of each eggplant slice (use slightly more filling for larger slices and slightly less for smaller slices). Gently roll up each eggplant slice and place seam side down in tomato sauce in skillet.
4. Heat broiler. Place skillet over medium heat, bring sauce to simmer, and cook for 5 minutes. Transfer skillet to oven and broil until eggplant is well browned and cheese is heated through, 5 to 10 minutes. Sprinkle with remaining ¼ cup Pecorino and let rest for 5 minutes. Sprinkle with remaining 1 tablespoon basil and serve.

Nutrition Info:

- Info430 cal., 31g fat (7g sag. fat), 30mg chol, 430mg sod., 28g carb (15g sugars, 12g fiber), 14g pro.

Sautéed Spinach With Chickpeas And Garlicky Yogurt

Servings: 4
Cooking Time: 45 Minutes

Ingredients:

- 1 cup plain low-fat yogurt
- 2 tablespoons chopped fresh mint
- 5 garlic cloves (4 sliced thin, 1 minced)
- 18 ounces (18 cups) baby spinach
- 2 tablespoons extra-virgin olive oil
- 1 teaspoon ground coriander
- 1 teaspoon ground turmeric
- ¼ teaspoon grated lemon zest
- ⅛ teaspoon red pepper flakes
- 2 (15-ounce) cans no-salt-added chickpeas, rinsed
- ½ cup oil-packed sun-dried tomatoes, sliced thin
- Salt and pepper

Directions:

1. Combine yogurt, mint, and minced garlic in bowl; cover and refrigerate sauce until ready to serve.
2. Microwave spinach and ¼ cup water in covered bowl until spinach is wilted and has reduced in volume by half, 3 to 4 minutes. Remove bowl from microwave and keep covered for 1 minute. Carefully transfer spinach to colander and, using back of rubber spatula, gently press spinach to release excess liquid. Transfer spinach to cutting board and chop coarsely. Return spinach to colander and press again.
3. Cook 1 tablespoon oil and sliced garlic in 12-inch skillet over medium heat, stirring constantly, until garlic is light golden brown and beginning to sizzle, 3 to 6 minutes. Stir in coriander, turmeric, lemon zest, and pepper flakes and cook until fragrant, about 30 seconds. Stir in chickpeas, tomatoes, and 2 tablespoons water. Cook, stirring occasionally, until water evaporates and tomatoes are softened, 1 to 245 minutes.
4. Stir in spinach and ¼ teaspoon salt and cook until uniformly wilted and glossy green, about 2 minutes. Transfer spinach mixture to serving platter, drizzle with remaining 1 tablespoon oil, and season with pepper to taste. Serve with yogurt sauce.

Nutrition Info:

- Info310 cal., 11g fat (2g sag. fat), 5mg chol, 360mg sod., 37g carb (5g sugars, 10g fiber), 15g pro.

Ricotta-stuffed Portobello Mushrooms

Servings: 6
Cooking Time: 30 Minutes

Ingredients:
- 3/4 cup reduced-fat ricotta cheese
- 3/4 cup grated Parmesan cheese, divided
- 1/2 cup shredded part-skim mozzarella cheese
- 2 tablespoons minced fresh parsley
- 1/8 teaspoon pepper
- 6 large portobello mushrooms
- 6 slices large tomato
- 3/4 cup fresh basil leaves
- 3 tablespoons slivered almonds or pine nuts, toasted
- 1 small garlic clove
- 2 tablespoons olive oil
- 2 to 3 teaspoons water

Directions:
1. In a small bowl, mix ricotta cheese, 1/4 cup Parmesan cheese, mozzarella cheese, parsley and pepper. Remove and discard stems from mushrooms; with a spoon, scrape and remove gills. Fill caps with ricotta mixture. Top with tomato slices.
2. Grill, covered, over medium heat 8-10 minutes or until mushrooms are tender. Remove from the grill with a metal spatula.
3. Meanwhile, place basil, almonds and garlic in a small food processor; pulse until chopped. Add remaining Parmesan cheese; pulse just until blended. While processing, gradually add the oil and enough water to reach the desired consistency. Spoon the mixture over stuffed mushrooms before serving.

Nutrition Info:
- Info201 cal., 13g fat (4g sat. fat), 22mg chol., 238mg sod., 9g carb. (5g sugars, 2g fiber), 12g pro.

"refried" Bean And Rice Casserole

Servings: 4
Cooking Time: 15 Minutes

Ingredients:
- 2 1/4 cups cooked brown rice (omit added salt or fat)
- 1 (15.5-ounce) can dark red kidney beans, rinsed and drained
- 7 tablespoons picante sauce
- 1/4 cup water
- 1/2 cup shredded, reduced-fat, sharp cheddar cheese

Directions:
1. Preheat the oven to 350°F.
2. Coat an 8-inch-square baking pan with nonstick cooking spray. Place the rice in the pan and set aside.
3. Add the beans, picante sauce, and water to a blender and blend until pureed, scraping the sides of the blender frequently.
4. Spread the bean mixture evenly over the rice and sprinkle with cheese. Bake, uncovered, for 15 minutes or until thoroughly heated.

Nutrition Info:
- Info260 cal., 3g fat (1g sag. fat), 5mg chol, 430mg sod., 44g carb (1g sugars, 7g fiber), 14g pro.

Tunisian-style Grilled Vegetables With Couscous And Eggs

Servings:6
Cooking Time:30 Minutes

Ingredients:
- DRESSING
- 2 teaspoons coriander seeds
- 1½ teaspoons caraway seeds
- 1 teaspoon cumin seeds
- 5 tablespoons extra-virgin olive oil
- ½ teaspoon paprika
- ⅛ teaspoon cayenne pepper
- 3 garlic cloves, minced
- ¼ cup chopped fresh parsley
- ¼ cup chopped fresh cilantro
- 2 tablespoons chopped fresh mint
- 1 teaspoon grated lemon zest plus 2 tablespoons juice
- Salt
- COUSCOUS AND VEGETABLES
- 1 tablespoon extra-virgin olive oil
- 1 cup whole-wheat couscous
- ¾ cup water
- ¾ cup low-sodium vegetable broth
- Salt and pepper
- 2 red or green bell peppers, tops and bottoms trimmed, stemmed and seeded, and peppers flattened
- 1 small eggplant, halved lengthwise and scored on cut sides
- 1 zucchini (8 to 10 ounces), halved lengthwise and scored on cut sides
- 4 plum tomatoes, cored and halved lengthwise
- 2 shallots, unpeeled
- 6 hard-cooked eggs, peeled and halved

Directions:
1. FOR THE DRESSING Grind coriander seeds, caraway seeds, and cumin seeds in spice grinder until finely ground. Whisk ground spices, oil, paprika, and cayenne together in bowl. Reserve 3 tablespoons spiced oil mixture for brushing vegetables before grilling. Heat remaining spiced oil and garlic in 8-inch skillet over low heat, stirring occasionally, until fragrant and small bubbles appear, 8 to 10 minutes. Transfer to large bowl, let cool for 10 minutes, then whisk in parsley, cilantro, mint, lemon zest and juice, and ¼ teaspoon salt; set aside for serving.
2. FOR THE COUSCOUS AND VEGETABLES Heat oil in saucepan over medium heat until shimmering. Add couscous and toast, stirring often, until a few grains begin to brown, about 3 minutes. Transfer couscous to large bowl. Add water, broth, and pinch salt to saucepan and bring to boil. Once boiling, immediately pour broth mixture over couscous, cover tightly with plastic wrap, and let sit until grains are tender, about 12 minutes. Fluff gently with fork to combine. Season with pepper to taste.
3. Meanwhile, brush interior of bell peppers and cut sides of eggplant, zucchini, and tomatoes with reserved oil mixture and sprinkle with ¼ teaspoon salt.
4. FOR A CHARCOAL GRILL Open bottom vent completely. Light large chimney starter three-quarters filled with charcoal briquettes (4½ quarts). When top coals are partially covered with ash, pour evenly over grill. Set cooking grate in place, cover, and open lid vent completely. Heat grill until hot, about 5 minutes.
5. FOR A GAS GRILL Turn all burners to high, cover, and heat grill until hot, about 15 minutes. Turn all burners to medium-high.
6. Clean and oil cooking grate. Place bell peppers, eggplant, zucchini, tomatoes, and shallots cut side down on grill. Cook (covered if using gas), turning as needed, until tender and slightly charred, 8 to 16 minutes. Transfer eggplant, zucchini, tomatoes, and shallots to baking sheet as they finish cooking; place bell peppers in bowl, cover with plastic wrap, and let steam to loosen skins.
7. Let vegetables cool slightly. Peel bell peppers, tomatoes, and shallots. Chop all vegetables into ½-inch pieces, then toss gently with dressing in bowl. Season with pepper to taste. Serve vegetables and hard-cooked eggs over couscous.

Nutrition Info:
- Info380 cal., 20g fat (3g sag. fat), 185mg chol, 300mg sod., 37g carb (10g sugars, 9g fiber), 13g pro.

Salads Recipes

Roasted Winter Squash Salad With Za'atar And Parsley

Servings:6
Cooking Time:45 Minutes
Ingredients:
- 3 pounds butternut squash, peeled, seeded, and cut into ½-inch pieces (8 cups)
- ¼ cup extra-virgin olive oil
- Salt and pepper
- 1½ teaspoons za'atar
- 1 small shallot, minced
- 2 tablespoons lemon juice
- ¾ cup fresh parsley leaves
- ⅓ cup roasted unsalted pepitas
- ½ cup pomegranate seeds

Directions:
1. Adjust oven rack to lowest position and heat oven to 450 degrees. Toss squash with 1 tablespoon oil and season with pepper. Arrange squash in single layer on rimmed baking sheet and roast until well browned and tender, 30 to 35 minutes, stirring halfway through roasting. Sprinkle squash with za'atar and let cool for 15 minutes. (Squash can be refrigerated for up to 24 hours; bring to room temperature before continuing.)
2. Whisk shallot, lemon juice, ¼ teaspoon salt, and remaining 3 tablespoons oil together in large bowl. Add squash, parsley, and pepitas and gently toss to coat. Sprinkle with pomegranate seeds. Serve.

Nutrition Info:
- Info230 cal., 13g fat (2g sag. fat), 0mg chol, 110mg sod., 27g carb (7g sugars, 5g fiber), 4g pro.

Broccoli & Apple Salad

Servings:6
Cooking Time: 15 Minutes
Ingredients:
- 3 cups small fresh broccoli florets
- 3 medium apples, chopped
- 1/2 cup chopped mixed dried fruit
- 1 tablespoon chopped red onion
- 1/2 cup reduced-fat plain yogurt
- 4 bacon strips, cooked and crumbled

Directions:
1. In a large bowl, combine broccoli, apples, dried fruit and onion. Add yogurt; toss to coat. Sprinkle with bacon. Refrigerate until serving.

Nutrition Info:
- Info124 cal., 3g fat (1g sat. fat), 7mg chol., 134mg sod., 22g carb. (17g sugars, 3g fiber), 4g pro.

Spicy Chipotle Chicken Salad With Corn

Servings: 6
Cooking Time: 60 Minutes

Ingredients:
- Salt and pepper
- 1½ pounds boneless, skinless chicken breasts, trimmed of all visible fat and pounded to ¾-inch thickness
- ⅓ cup mayonnaise
- 3 tablespoons lime juice (2 limes)
- 2 teaspoons minced canned chipotle chile in adobo sauce
- 1 teaspoon extra-virgin olive oil
- 1 red bell pepper, stemmed, seeded, and chopped fine
- ⅓ cup frozen corn, thawed
- 2 scallions, minced
- 2 tablespoons minced fresh cilantro

Directions:
1. Whisk 4 quarts water and 2 tablespoons salt in Dutch oven until salt is dissolved. Arrange breasts, skinned side up, in steamer basket, making sure not to overlap them. Submerge steamer basket in water.
2. Heat pot over medium heat, stirring liquid occasionally to even out hot spots, until water registers 175 degrees, 15 to 20 minutes. Turn off heat, cover pot, remove from burner, and let sit until meat registers 160 degrees, 17 to 22 minutes. Transfer chicken to paper towel–lined plate and refrigerate until cool, about 30 minutes.
3. Whisk mayonnaise, lime juice, chipotle, oil, ¼ teaspoon salt, and ¼ teaspoon pepper in large bowl until combined. Pat chicken dry with paper towels and cut into ½-inch pieces. Add chicken, bell pepper, corn, scallions, and cilantro to mayonnaise mixture and gently toss to coat. (Salad can be refrigerated for up to 2 days.) Season with pepper to taste. Serve.

Nutrition Info:
- Info240 cal., 13g fat (2g sag. fat), 85mg chol, 280mg sod., 4g carb (1g sugars, 1g fiber), 26g pro.

Tangy Sweet Carrot Pepper Salad

Servings: 4
Cooking Time: 1 Minute

Ingredients:
- 1 1/2 cups peeled sliced carrots (about 1/8-inch thick)
- 2 tablespoons water
- 3/4 cup thinly sliced green bell pepper
- 1/3 cup thinly sliced onion
- 1/4 cup reduced-fat Catalina dressing

Directions:
1. Place carrots and water in a shallow, microwave-safe dish, such as a glass pie plate. Cover with plastic wrap and microwave on HIGH for 1 minute or until carrots are just tender-crisp. Be careful not to overcook them—the carrots should retain some crispness.
2. Immediately place the carrots in a colander and run under cold water about 30 seconds to cool. Shake to drain and place the carrots on paper towels to dry further. Dry the dish.
3. When the carrots are completely cool, return them to the dish, add the remaining ingredients, and toss gently to coat.
4. Serve immediately, or chill 30 minutes for a more blended flavor. Flavors are at their peak if you serve this salad within 30 minutes of adding dressing.

Nutrition Info:
- Info60 cal., 0g fat (0g sag. fat), 0mg chol, 200mg sod., 11g carb (7g sugars, 2g fiber), 1g pro.

Classic Wedge Salad

Servings:6
Cooking Time:15minutes
Ingredients:
- 3 slices uncured bacon, cut into ¼-inch pieces
- ⅓ cup buttermilk
- 1 ounce strong blue cheese, such as Roquefort or Stilton, crumbled (¼ cup)
- ⅓ cup mayonnaise
- ⅓ cup low-fat sour cream
- 3 tablespoons water
- 1 tablespoon white wine vinegar
- ¼ teaspoon garlic powder
- ¼ teaspoon pepper
- 1 head iceberg lettuce (2 pounds), cored and cut into 6 wedges
- 3 tomatoes, cored and cut into ½-inch-thick wedges
- 2 tablespoons minced fresh chives

Directions:
1. Cook bacon in 12-inch nonstick skillet over medium-high heat until rendered and crisp, about 5 minutes. Using slotted spoon, transfer bacon to paper towel–lined plate.
2. Mash buttermilk and blue cheese together with fork in small bowl until mixture resembles cottage cheese with small curds. Stir in mayonnaise, sour cream, water, vinegar, garlic powder, and pepper until combined.
3. Divide lettuce and tomatoes among individual plates. Spoon dressing over top, then sprinkle with bacon and chives. Serve.

Nutrition Info:
- Info170 cal., 13g fat (3g sag. fat), 15mg chol, 270mg sod., 7g carb (5g sugars, 2g fiber), 6g pro.

Garden Bounty Potato Salad

Servings:20
Cooking Time: 25 Minutes
Ingredients:
- 3 pounds small red potatoes, quartered
- 1 pound fresh green beans, trimmed and cut in half
- 1/3 cup olive oil
- 1/4 cup red wine vinegar
- 1/4 cup minced fresh basil
- 2 tablespoons minced fresh parsley
- 1 1/2 teaspoons salt
- 1/2 teaspoon pepper
- 6 hard-cooked large eggs, sliced
- 1 cup grape tomatoes

Directions:
1. Place potatoes in a large saucepan and cover with water. Bring to a boil. Reduce heat; cover and cook for 10-15 minutes or until tender, adding beans during the last 4 minutes of cooking. Drain. Transfer to a large bowl.
2. In a small bowl, whisk oil, vinegar, basil, parsley, salt and pepper. Pour over potato mixture; toss to coat. Cover and refrigerate for at least 1 hour.
3. Stir before serving; top with eggs and tomatoes.

Nutrition Info:
- Info113 cal., 5g fat (1g sat. fat), 64mg chol., 202mg sod., 13g carb. (2g sugars, 2g fiber), 4g pro.

Shrimp Salad With Avocado And Grapefruit

Servings: 4
Cooking Time: 10 Minutes
Ingredients:
- 1 lemon, halved
- 1 bay leaf
- ½ teaspoon peppercorns
- 1 pound extra-large shrimp (21 to 25 per pound), peeled, deveined, and tails removed
- 1 grapefruit
- 1 avocado, halved, pitted, and cut into ½-inch pieces
- 3 tablespoons lime juice
- 1½ teaspoons grated fresh ginger
- ½ teaspoon honey
- ¼ teaspoon pepper
- ⅛ teaspoon salt
- 2 ounces snow peas, strings removed and sliced thin lengthwise
- 1 tablespoon chopped fresh mint
- 2 small heads Bibb lettuce (12 ounces), leaves separated and torn into bite-size pieces
- 2 tablespoons extra-virgin olive oil

Directions:
1. Place 3 cups water in medium saucepan. Squeeze lemon halves into water, then add spent halves, bay leaf, and peppercorns. Bring to boil over high heat and cook for 2 minutes.
2. Off heat, add shrimp. Cover and let steep until shrimp are firm and pink, about 7 minutes. Fill large bowl halfway with ice and water. Drain shrimp, discarding lemon halves and bay leaf, and transfer to prepared ice bath. Let sit until chilled, about 2 minutes. Transfer shrimp to paper towel–lined plate. (Shrimp can be refrigerated for up to 24 hours.)
3. Cut away peel and pith from grapefruit. Holding fruit over fine-mesh strainer set in bowl, use paring knife to slice between membranes to release segments. Measure out and reserve ¼ cup juice; discard remaining juice. Process reserved grapefruit juice, one-quarter of avocado, 2 tablespoons lime juice, ginger, honey, pepper, and salt in blender until smooth; transfer dressing to large bowl.
4. Add shrimp, grapefruit segments, snow peas, mint, and remaining avocado to bowl with dressing and gently toss to coat. Combine lettuce, oil, and remaining 1 tablespoon lime juice in separate bowl and gently toss to coat. Arrange lettuce on individual plates and top with shrimp mixture. Drizzle with any dressing remaining in bowl and serve.

Nutrition Info:
- Info260 cal., 15g fat (2g sag. fat), 105mg chol, 210mg sod., 18g carb (8g sugars, 4g fiber), 15g pro.

Michigan Cherry Salad

Servings: 8
Cooking Time: 15 Minutes
Ingredients:
- 7 ounces fresh baby spinach (about 9 cups)
- 3 ounces spring mix salad greens (about 5 cups)
- 1 large apple, chopped
- 1/2 cup coarsely chopped pecans, toasted
- 1/2 cup dried cherries
- 1/4 cup crumbled Gorgonzola cheese
- DRESSING
- 1/4 cup fresh raspberries
- 1/4 cup red wine vinegar
- 3 tablespoons cider vinegar
- 3 tablespoons cherry preserves
- 1 tablespoon sugar
- 2 tablespoons olive oil

Directions:
1. In a large bowl, combine the first six ingredients.
2. Place the raspberries, vinegars, preserves and sugar in a blender. While processing, gradually add oil in a steady stream. Drizzle over salad; toss to coat.

Nutrition Info:
- Info172 cal., 10g fat (2g sat. fat), 3mg chol., 78mg sod., 21g carb. (16g sugars, 3g fiber), 3g pro.

Toasted Pecan And Apple Salad

Servings: 4
Cooking Time: 8 Minutes

Ingredients:
- 2 tablespoons pecan chips
- 2 cups chopped unpeeled red apples
- 1/4 cup dried raisin-cherry blend (or 1/4 cup dried cherries or golden raisins alone)
- 1 teaspoon honey (or 1 teaspoon packed dark brown sugar and 1 teaspoon water)

Directions:
1. Place a small skillet over medium-high heat until hot. Add the pecans and cook 1–2 minutes or until beginning to lightly brown, stirring constantly. Remove from the heat and set aside on paper towels to stop the cooking process and cool quickly.
2. Combine the apples and dried fruit in a medium bowl, drizzle honey over all, and toss gently.
3. Serve on a lettuce leaf (if desired) or a pretty salad plate. Sprinkle each serving evenly with the pecans.

Nutrition Info:
- Info90 cal., 2g fat (0g sag. fat), 0mg chol, 0mg sod., 18g carb (14g sugars, 2g fiber), 1g pro.

Warm Cabbage Salad With Chicken

Servings:6
Cooking Time:40 Minutes

Ingredients:
- DRESSING AND CHICKEN
- Salt
- 1½ pounds boneless, skinless chicken breasts, trimmed of all visible fat and pounded to 1-inch thickness
- 3 tablespoons canola oil
- 1 tablespoon grated fresh ginger
- 2 garlic cloves, minced
- 5 tablespoons rice vinegar
- 2 tablespoons fish sauce
- 1–2 teaspoons Asian chili-garlic sauce
- SALAD
- ½ head napa cabbage, cored and sliced thin (5½ cups)
- 2 carrots, peeled and shredded
- 4 scallions, sliced thin on bias
- ½ cup fresh cilantro leaves
- ½ cup minced fresh mint
- 3 tablespoons coarsely chopped dry-roasted unsalted peanuts

Directions:
1. FOR THE DRESSING AND CHICKEN Whisk 4 quarts water and 2 tablespoons salt in Dutch oven until salt is dissolved. Arrange breasts, skinned side up, in steamer basket, making sure not to overlap them. Submerge steamer basket in water.
2. Heat pot over medium heat, stirring liquid occasionally to even out hot spots, until water registers 175 degrees, 15 to 20 minutes. Turn off heat, cover pot, remove from burner, and let sit until meat registers 160 degrees, 17 to 22 minutes. Transfer chicken to paper towel–lined plate and refrigerate until cool, about 30 minutes. (Chicken can be refrigerated for up to 2 days.)
3. Pat chicken dry with paper towels and shred into bite-size pieces with 2 forks. Heat oil in 12-inch skillet over medium heat until shimmering. Add ginger and garlic and cook until fragrant, about 30 seconds. Whisk in vinegar, fish sauce, and chili-garlic sauce and bring to simmer. Add chicken and cook until heated through, about 1 minute.
4. FOR THE SALAD Combine all ingredients in large bowl. Add chicken mixture and gently toss to coat. Serve immediately.

Nutrition Info:
- Info270 cal., 12g fat (1g sag. fat), 85mg chol, 380mg sod., 8g carb (3g sugars, 3g fiber), 29g pro.

Walnut Vinaigrette

Servings:1
Cooking Time:8 Minutes
Ingredients:
- 1 tablespoon white wine vinegar
- 1½ teaspoons minced shallot
- ½ teaspoon mayonnaise
- ½ teaspoon Dijon mustard
- ⅛ teaspoon salt
- Pinch pepper
- 1½ tablespoons roasted walnut oil
- 1½ tablespoons extra-virgin olive oil

Directions:
1. Whisk vinegar, shallot, mayonnaise, mustard, salt, and pepper together in bowl. While whisking constantly, drizzle in oils until completely emulsified. (Vinaigrette can be refrigerated for up to 1 week; whisk to recombine.)

Nutrition Info:
- Info100 cal., 11g fat (1g sag. fat), 0mg chol, 90mg sod., 0g carb (0g sugars, 0g fiber), 0g pro.

Arugula Salad With Fennel And Shaved Parmesan

Servings:6
Cooking Time:12minutes
Ingredients:
- 1½ tablespoons lemon juice
- 1 small shallot, minced
- 1 teaspoon Dijon mustard
- 1 teaspoon minced fresh thyme
- 1 small garlic clove, minced
- Salt and pepper
- ¼ cup extra-virgin olive oil
- 6 ounces (6 cups) baby arugula
- 1 large fennel bulb, stalks discarded, bulb halved, cored, and sliced thin
- 1 ounce Parmesan cheese, shaved

Directions:
1. Whisk lemon juice, shallot, mustard, thyme, garlic, ⅛ teaspoon salt, and pinch pepper together in large bowl. While whisking constantly, drizzle in oil until completely emulsified. Add arugula and fennel and gently toss to coat. Season with pepper to taste. Sprinkle with Parmesan. Serve.

Nutrition Info:
- Info130 cal., 11g fat (2g sag. fat), 5mg chol, 190mg sod., 6g carb (3g sugars, 2g fiber), 4g pro.

Brussels Sprout Salad With Pecorino And Pine Nuts

Servings:6
Cooking Time: 2 Hours
Ingredients:
- 2 tablespoons lemon juice
- 1 tablespoon Dijon mustard
- 1 small shallot, minced
- 1 garlic clove, minced
- Salt and pepper
- ¼ cup extra-virgin olive oil
- 1 pound Brussels sprouts, trimmed, halved, and sliced very thin
- 1 ounce Pecorino Romano cheese, shredded (⅓ cup)
- ¼ cup pine nuts, toasted

Directions:
1. Whisk lemon juice, mustard, shallot, garlic, and ⅛ teaspoon salt in large bowl until combined. While whisking constantly, drizzle in oil until completely emulsified. Add Brussels sprouts, gently toss to coat, and let sit for at least 30 minutes or up to 2 hours.
2. Stir in Pecorino and pine nuts. Season with pepper to taste. Serve.

Nutrition Info:
- Info170 cal., 15g fat (2g sag. fat), 5mg chol, 190mg sod., 8g carb (2g sugars, 3g fiber), 5g pro.

Warm Spinach Salad With Apple, Blue Cheese, And Pecans

Servings:6
Cooking Time:10 Minutes
Ingredients:
- 1½ ounces blue cheese, crumbled (⅓ cup)
- 3 tablespoons extra-virgin olive oil
- 1 (3-inch) strip orange zest plus 1 tablespoon juice
- 1 shallot, minced
- 1 teaspoon white vinegar
- 10 ounces curly-leaf spinach, stemmed and torn into bite-size pieces
- ½ Fuji, Gala, or Golden Delicious apple, cored and cut into ½-inch pieces
- 3 tablespoons chopped toasted pecans
- Pepper

Directions:
1. Place blue cheese on plate and freeze until slightly firm, about 15 minutes.
2. Cook oil, orange zest, and shallot in Dutch oven over medium-low heat until shallot is softened, about 5 minutes. Off heat, discard zest and stir in orange juice and vinegar. Add spinach, cover, and let sit until just beginning to wilt, about 30 seconds.
3. Transfer spinach mixture and liquid left in pot to large bowl. Add apple, pecans, and blue cheese and gently toss to coat. Season with pepper to taste. Serve.

Nutrition Info:
- Info130 cal., 12g fat (2g sag. fat), 5mg chol, 120mg sod., 5g carb (2g sugars, 2g fiber), 3g pro.

Meat Recipes

Peppered Beef Tenderloin

Servings:12
Cooking Time: 40 Minutes
Ingredients:
- 3 tablespoons coarsely ground pepper
- 2 tablespoons olive oil
- 1 tablespoon grated lemon peel
- 2 garlic cloves, minced
- 1 teaspoon salt
- 1 beef tenderloin roast (3 to 4 pounds)

Directions:
1. Preheat oven to 400°. Mix the first five ingredients.
2. Place roast on a rack in a roasting pan; rub with pepper mixture. Roast until desired doneness (for medium-rare, a thermometer should read 145°; medium, 160°; well-done, 170°), 40-60 minutes. Remove roast from oven; tent with foil. Let roast stand 15 minutes before slicing.

Nutrition Info:
- Info188 cal., 9g fat (3g sat. fat), 49mg chol., 197mg sod., 1g carb. (0 sugars, 1g fiber), 24g pro.

Cajun Beef & Rice

Servings:4
Cooking Time: 30 Minutes
Ingredients:
- 1 pound lean ground beef (90% lean)
- 3 celery ribs, chopped
- 1 small green pepper, chopped
- 1 small sweet red pepper, chopped
- 1/4 cup chopped onion
- 2 cups water
- 1 cup instant brown rice
- 1 tablespoon minced fresh parsley
- 1 tablespoon Worcestershire sauce
- 2 teaspoons reduced-sodium beef bouillon granules
- 1 teaspoon Cajun seasoning
- 1/4 teaspoon crushed red pepper flakes
- 1/4 teaspoon pepper
- 1/8 teaspoon garlic powder

Directions:
1. In a large skillet, cook beef, celery, green and red peppers, and onion over medium heat 8-10 minutes or until beef is no longer pink, breaking up beef into crumbles; drain.
2. Stir in remaining ingredients. Bring to a boil. Reduce heat; simmer, covered, 12-15 minutes or until rice is tender.

Nutrition Info:
- Info291 cal., 10g fat (4g sat. fat), 71mg chol., 422mg sod., 23g carb. (3g sugars, 2g fiber), 25g pro.

Spinach Steak Pinwheels

Servings: 6
Cooking Time: 25 Minutes

Ingredients:

- 1 1/2 pounds beef top sirloin steak
- 8 bacon strips, cooked
- 1 package (10 ounces) frozen chopped spinach, thawed and squeezed dry
- 1/4 cup grated Parmesan cheese
- 1/2 teaspoon salt
- 1/8 teaspoon cayenne pepper

Directions:

1. Lightly score the steak by making shallow diagonal cuts at 1-in. intervals into top of steak; repeat cuts in the opposite direction. Cover steak with plastic wrap; pound with a meat mallet to 1/2-in. thickness. Remove plastic.
2. Place bacon widthwise at center of steak. In a bowl, mix the remaining ingredients; spoon over bacon. Starting at a short side, roll up steak jelly-roll style; secure with toothpicks. Cut into six slices.
3. Lightly coat grill rack with cooking oil. Grill pinwheels, covered, over medium heat 5-6 minutes on each side or until beef reaches desired doneness (for medium-rare, a thermometer should read 145°; medium, 160°). Discard toothpicks before serving.

Nutrition Info:

- Info227 cal., 10g fat (4g sat. fat), 60mg chol., 536mg sod., 3g carb. (0 sugars, 1g fiber), 31g pro.

Smoky Sirloin

Servings: 4
Cooking Time: 12 Minutes

Ingredients:

- 1 pound boneless sirloin steak, about 3/4-inch thick
- 1 1/2 teaspoons smoked paprika
- 2 tablespoons Worcestershire sauce
- 2 tablespoons balsamic vinegar

Directions:

1. Sprinkle both sides of the beef with paprika, 1/4 teaspoon salt, and 1/4 teaspoon pepper. Press down lightly to adhere. Let stand 15 minutes at room temperature.
2. Heat a large skillet coated with cooking spray over medium-high heat. Cook beef 4 to 5 minutes on each side. Place on cutting board and let stand 5 minutes before slicing.
3. Combine 1/4 cup water, Worcestershire sauce, and vinegar. Pour into the skillet with any pan residue and bring to a boil over medium-high heat. Boil 2 minutes or until reduced to 2 tablespoons liquid. Pour over sliced beef.

Nutrition Info:

- Info150 cal., 3g fat (1g sag. fat), 70mg chol, 280mg sod., 3g carb (2g sugars, 0g fiber), 26g pro.

Chili Sloppy Joes

Servings: 6
Cooking Time: 20 Minutes

Ingredients:

- 1 pound lean ground beef (90% lean)
- 1 cup finely chopped sweet onion
- 1/2 cup finely chopped green pepper
- 1 jalapeno pepper, seeded and finely chopped, optional
- 1/2 cup chili sauce
- 1/2 cup water
- 1 to 2 chipotle peppers in adobo sauce, finely chopped
- 1 tablespoon packed brown sugar
- 1 teaspoon yellow mustard
- 6 kaiser rolls or hamburger buns, split
- 2 tablespoons butter, softened
- Pickle slices, optional

Directions:

1. Preheat broiler. In a large skillet, cook beef, onion, green pepper and if desired, jalapeno, over medium heat 5-7 minutes or until beef is no longer pink, breaking up beef into crumbles; drain.
2. Stir in chili sauce, water, chipotle peppers, brown sugar and mustard; bring to a boil. Simmer, uncovered, 8-10 minutes or until slightly thickened, stirring occasionally.
3. Spread cut sides of rolls with butter; arrange on a baking sheet, buttered side up. Broil 3-4 in. from heat until lightly toasted, about 30 seconds. Fill with beef mixture and, if desired, pickles.

Nutrition Info:

- Info313 cal., 12g fat (5g sat. fat), 57mg chol., 615mg sod., 32g carb. (11g sugars, 2g fiber), 19g pro.

Cabbage Roll Skillet

Servings: 6
Cooking Time: 20 Minutes

Ingredients:

- 1 can (28 ounces) whole plum tomatoes, undrained
- 1 pound extra-lean ground beef (95% lean)
- 1 large onion, chopped
- 1 can (8 ounces) tomato sauce
- 2 tablespoons cider vinegar
- 1 tablespoon brown sugar
- 1 teaspoon dried oregano
- 1 teaspoon dried thyme
- 1/2 teaspoon pepper
- 1 small head cabbage, thinly sliced (about 6 cups)
- 1 medium green pepper, cut into thin strips
- 4 cups hot cooked brown rice

Directions:

1. Drain tomatoes, reserving liquid; coarsely chop tomatoes. In a large nonstick skillet, cook beef and onion over medium-high heat 6-8 minutes or until beef is no longer pink, breaking up beef into crumbles. Stir in the tomato sauce, vinegar, brown sugar, seasonings, chopped tomatoes and reserved liquid.
2. Add cabbage and pepper; cook, covered, 6 minutes, stirring mixture occasionally. Cook, uncovered, 6-8 minutes or until cabbage is tender. Serve with rice.

Nutrition Info:

- Info332 cal., 5g fat (2g sat. fat), 43mg chol., 439mg sod., 50g carb. (12g sugars, 9g fiber), 22g pro.

One-pot Beef & Pepper Stew

Servings: 8
Cooking Time: 30 Minutes
Ingredients:
- 1 pound lean ground beef (90% lean)
- 3 cans (14 1/2 ounces each) diced tomatoes, undrained
- 4 large green peppers, coarsely chopped
- 1 large onion, chopped
- 2 cans (4 ounces each) chopped green chilies
- 3 teaspoons garlic powder
- 1 teaspoon pepper
- 1/4 teaspoon salt
- 2 cups uncooked instant rice
- Hot pepper sauce, optional

Directions:
1. In a 6-qt. stockpot, cook beef over medium heat 6-8 minutes or until no longer pink, breaking into crumbles; drain. Add tomatoes, green peppers, onion, chilies and seasonings; bring to a boil. Reduce heat; simmer, covered, for 20-25 minutes or until vegetables are tender.
2. Prepare rice according to package directions. Serve with the stew and, if desired, pepper sauce.

Nutrition Info:
- Info244 cal., 5g fat (2g sat. fat), 35mg chol., 467mg sod., 35g carb. (8g sugars, 5g fiber), 15g pro.

Cumin'd Beef Patties And Santa Fe Sour Cream

Servings: 4
Cooking Time: 8 Minutes
Ingredients:
- 1 pound 96% lean ground beef
- 1/3 cup mild picante sauce (divided use)
- 2 teaspoons ground cumin
- 1/8 teaspoon salt (divided use)
- 1/8 teaspoon black pepper
- 1/4 cup fat-free sour cream
- 2 whole-wheat hamburger buns

Directions:
1. Mix the ground beef, all but 2 tablespoons of the picante sauce, cumin, 1/16 teaspoon salt, and black pepper in a medium bowl until well blended. Shape the beef mixture into 4 patties.
2. Place a large nonstick skillet over medium-high heat until hot. Coat the skillet with nonstick cooking spray, add the patties, and cook 4 minutes. Flip the patties and cook another 3 minutes or until they are no longer pink in the center.
3. Meanwhile, stir 2 tablespoons picante sauce, 1/16 teaspoon salt, and the sour cream together in a small bowl.
4. Serve each patty on 1/2 of a hamburger bun and top with 1 1/2 tablespoons sour cream. Spoon an additional 1/2 teaspoon picante sauce on top of each serving, if desired.

Nutrition Info:
- Info230 cal., 6g fat (2g sag. fat), 65mg chol, 460mg sod., 15g carb (3g sugars, 2g fiber), 29g pro.

Steak Tacos With Jícama Slaw

Servings: 4
Cooking Time: 30 Seconds
Ingredients:
- SLAW
- 1 pound jícama, peeled and cut into 3-inch-long matchsticks
- ¼ cup thinly sliced red onion
- 3 tablespoons chopped fresh cilantro
- 1 tablespoon extra-virgin olive oil
- 1 teaspoon grated lime zest plus 2 tablespoons juice
- ¼ teaspoon salt
- TACOS
- ½ cup fresh cilantro leaves
- 3 scallions, chopped
- 3 garlic cloves, peeled
- 1 jalapeño chile, stemmed, seeded, and chopped
- ½ teaspoon ground cumin
- 2 tablespoons extra-virgin olive oil
- 1 tablespoon lime juice
- 1 (1-pound) flank steak, trimmed of all visible fat and cut lengthwise into 3 equal pieces
- Salt and pepper
- 12 (6-inch) corn tortillas, warmed

Directions:
1. FOR THE SLAW Combine all ingredients in bowl. Cover and refrigerate until ready to serve.
2. FOR THE TACOS Pulse cilantro, scallions, garlic, jalapeño, cumin, and 4 teaspoons oil in food processor to paste, 10 to 12 pulses, scraping down sides of bowl as needed. Transfer 2 tablespoons herb paste to bowl, whisk in lime juice, and set aside for serving.
3. Using fork, poke each piece of steak 10 to 12 times on each side. Sprinkle steaks with ¼ teaspoon salt and place in 13 by 9-inch baking dish. Coat steaks thoroughly with remaining herb paste, cover dish, and refrigerate at least 30 minutes or up to 1 hour.
4. Scrape herb paste off steaks and pat dry with paper towels. Heat remaining 2 teaspoons oil in 12-inch nonstick skillet over medium-high heat until just smoking. Cook steaks until well browned and meat registers 120 to 125 degrees (for medium-rare), 5 to 7 minutes per side, adjusting heat as needed to prevent scorching. Transfer steaks to carving board and let rest for 5 minutes.
5. Slice steaks thin against grain on bias and transfer to large bowl. Toss steak with reserved herb mixture and season with pepper to taste. Divide steak evenly among tortillas and top with slaw. Serve.

Nutrition Info:
- Info480 cal., 19g fat (4g sag. fat), 70mg chol, 370mg sod., 47g carb (3g sugars, 9g fiber), 29g pro.

Sweet Jerk Pork

Servings: 4
Cooking Time: 20 Minutes
Ingredients:
- 1 pound pork tenderloin
- 2 teaspoons jerk seasoning
- 2 tablespoons packed dark brown sugar
- 2 teaspoons Worcestershire sauce

Directions:
1. Preheat the oven to 425°F.
2. Sprinkle the pork evenly with the jerk seasoning and press down gently so the spices adhere. Let the pork stand 15 minutes.
3. Stir the sugar and Worcestershire sauce together in a small bowl until well blended. Coat an 11 × 7-inch baking pan with nonstick cooking spray and set aside.
4. Place a large nonstick skillet over medium-high heat until hot. Coat the skillet with nonstick cooking spray, add the pork, and brown all sides, about 5 minutes, turning occasionally.
5. Place the pork in the baking pan and spoon all but 1 tablespoon of the Worcestershire mixture evenly over the pork. Bake for 13–15 minutes or until the pork is barely pink in the center and a meat thermometer reaches 170°F.
6. Place the pork on a cutting board, spoon the remaining 1 tablespoon Worcestershire mixture evenly over all, and let stand 10 minutes before slicing.

Nutrition Info:
- Info150 cal., 3g fat (1g sag. fat), 60mg chol, 210mg sod., 8g carb (8g sugars, 0g fiber), 22g pro.

Quick Hawaiian Pizza

Servings: 6
Cooking Time: 25 Minutes

Ingredients:

- 1 prebaked 12-inch thin whole wheat pizza crust
- 1/2 cup marinara sauce
- 1/4 cup barbecue sauce
- 1 medium sweet yellow or red pepper, chopped
- 1 cup cubed fresh pineapple
- 1/2 cup chopped fully cooked ham
- 1 cup shredded part-skim mozzarella cheese
- 1/2 cup shredded cheddar cheese

Directions:

1. Preheat oven to 425°. Place crust on a baking sheet. Mix marinara and barbecue sauces; spread over crust.
2. Top with remaining ingredients. Bake until crust is browned and cheeses are melted, 10-15 minutes.

Nutrition Info:

- Info290 cal., 10g fat (5g sat. fat), 29mg chol., 792mg sod., 36g carb. (11g sugars, 5g fiber), 16g pro.

Braised Pork Stew

Servings: 4
Cooking Time: 30 Minutes

Ingredients:

- 1 pound pork tenderloin, cut into 1-inch cubes
- 1/2 teaspoon salt
- 1/2 teaspoon pepper
- 5 tablespoons all-purpose flour, divided
- 1 tablespoon olive oil
- 1 package (16 ounces) frozen vegetables for stew
- 1 1/2 cups reduced-sodium chicken broth
- 2 garlic cloves, minced
- 2 teaspoons stone-ground mustard
- 1 teaspoon dried thyme
- 2 tablespoons water

Directions:

1. Sprinkle pork with salt and pepper; add 3 tablespoons flour and toss to coat. In a large skillet, heat oil over medium heat. Brown pork. Drain if necessary. Stir in vegetables, broth, garlic, mustard and thyme. Bring to a boil. Reduce heat; simmer, covered, for 10-15 minutes or until pork and vegetables are tender.
2. In a small bowl, mix remaining flour and water until smooth; stir into stew. Return to a boil, stirring constantly; cook and stir 1-2 minutes or until stew is thickened.

Nutrition Info:

- Info275 cal., 8g fat (2g sat. fat), 63mg chol., 671mg sod., 24g carb. (2g sugars, 1g fiber), 26g pro.

Sunday Pork Roast

Servings: 12
Cooking Time: 1 Hour 10 Minutes
Ingredients:
- 2 medium onions, chopped
- 2 medium carrots, chopped
- 1 celery rib, chopped
- 4 tablespoons all-purpose flour, divided
- 1 bay leaf, finely crushed
- 1/2 teaspoon dried thyme
- 1 1/4 teaspoons salt, divided
- 1 1/4 teaspoons pepper, divided
- 1 boneless pork loin roast (3 to 4 pounds)
- 1/3 cup packed brown sugar

Directions:
1. Preheat oven to 350°. Place the vegetables on bottom of a shallow roasting pan. Mix 2 tablespoons flour, bay leaf, thyme and 1 teaspoon each salt and pepper; rub over roast. Place roast on top of vegetables, fat side up. Add 1 cup water to pan.
2. Roast 1 hour, basting once with pan juices if desired. Sprinkle brown sugar over roast. Roast 10-15 minutes longer or until a thermometer reads 140°. (Temperature of roast will continue to rise about 5-10° upon standing.)
3. Remove roast to a platter. Tent with foil; let stand 15 minutes before slicing.
4. Strain drippings from roasting pan into a measuring cup; skim off fat. Add enough water to drippings to measure 1 1/2 cups.
5. In a small saucepan over medium heat, whisk remaining flour and 1/3 cup water until smooth. Gradually whisk in drippings mixture and remaining salt and pepper. Bring gravy to a boil over medium-high heat, stirring constantly; cook and stir for 2 minutes or until thickened. Serve roast with gravy.

Nutrition Info:
- Info174 cal., 5g fat (2g sat. fat), 57mg chol., 280mg sod., 8g carb. (6g sugars, 0 fiber), 22g pro.

Spicy Chili'd Sirloin Steak

Servings: 4
Cooking Time: 11 Minutes
Ingredients:
- 1 pound boneless sirloin steak, trimmed of fat
- 2 tablespoons chili seasoning (available in packets)
- 1/8 teaspoon salt

Directions:
1. Coat both sides of the sirloin with the chili seasoning mix, pressing down so the spices adhere. Let stand 15 minutes, or overnight in the refrigerator for a spicier flavor (let steak stand at room temperature 15 minutes before cooking).
2. Place a large nonstick skillet over medium-high heat until hot. Coat the skillet with nonstick cooking spray, add the beef, and cook 5 minutes. Turn the steak, reduce the heat to medium, cover tightly, and cook 5 minutes. Do not overcook. Remove the skillet from the heat and let stand 2 minutes, covered.
3. Sprinkle the steak with salt and cut into 1/4-inch slices. Pour any accumulated juices over the steak slices.

Nutrition Info:
- Info140 cal., 4g fat (1g sag. fat), 40mg chol, 250mg sod., 2g carb (0g sugars, 0g fiber), 23g pro.

Special Treats Recipes

Frozen Chocolate Monkey Treats

Servings:1
Cooking Time: 20 Minutes
Ingredients:
- 3 medium bananas
- 1 cup (6 ounces) dark chocolate chips
- 2 teaspoons shortening
- Toppings: chopped peanuts, toasted flaked coconut and/or colored jimmies

Directions:
1. Cut each banana into six pieces (about 1 in.). Insert a toothpick into each piece; transfer to a waxed paper-lined baking sheet. Freeze until completely firm, about 1 hour.
2. In a microwave, melt chocolate and shortening; stir until smooth. Dip banana pieces in chocolate mixture; allow excess to drip off. Dip in toppings as desired; return to baking sheet. Freeze 30 minutes before serving.

Nutrition Info:
- Info72 cal., 4g fat (2g sat. fat), 0 chol., 0 sod., 10g carb. (7g sugars, 1g fiber), 1g pro.

Lemon Cupcakes With Strawberry Frosting

Servings:2
Cooking Time: 25 Minutes
Ingredients:
- 1 package white cake mix (regular size)
- 1/4 cup lemon curd
- 3 tablespoons lemon juice
- 3 teaspoons grated lemon peel
- 1/2 cup butter, softened
- 3 1/2 cups confectioners' sugar
- 1/4 cup seedless strawberry jam
- 2 tablespoons 2% milk
- 1 cup sliced fresh strawberries

Directions:
1. Line 24 muffin cups with paper liners. Prepare cake mix batter according to package directions, decreasing water by 1 tablespoon and adding lemon curd, lemon juice and lemon peel before mixing batter. Fill the prepared cups about two-thirds full. Bake and cool cupcakes as the package directs.
2. In a large bowl, beat the butter, confectioners' sugar, jam and milk until smooth. Frost cooled cupcakes; top with strawberries. Refrigerate leftovers.

Nutrition Info:
- Info219 cal., 7g fat (3g sat. fat), 13mg chol., 171mg sod., 23g carb. (29g sugars, 0 fiber), 1g pro.

Chocolate-dipped Strawberry Meringue Roses

Servings: 3
Cooking Time: 40 Minutes

Ingredients:

- 3 large egg whites
- 1/4 cup sugar
- 1/4 cup freeze-dried strawberries
- 1 package (3 ounces) strawberry gelatin
- 1/2 teaspoon vanilla extract, optional
- 1 cup 60% cacao bittersweet chocolate baking chips, melted

Directions:

1. Place egg whites in a large bowl; let stand at room temperature 30 minutes. Preheat oven to 225°.
2. Place sugar and strawberries in a food processor; process until powdery. Add gelatin; pulse to blend.
3. Beat egg whites on medium speed until foamy, adding vanilla if desired. Gradually add gelatin mixture, 1 tablespoon at a time, beating on high after each addition until sugar is dissolved. Continue beating until stiff glossy peaks form.
4. Cut a small hole in the tip of a pastry bag or in a corner of a food-safe plastic bag; insert a #1M star tip. Transfer meringue to bag. Pipe 2-in. roses 1 1/2 in. apart onto parchment paper-lined baking sheets.
5. Bake 40-45 minutes or until set and dry. Turn off oven (do not open oven door); leave meringues in oven 1 1/2 hours. Remove from oven; cool completely on baking sheets.
6. Remove meringues from paper. Dip bottoms in melted chocolate; allow excess to drip off. Place on waxed paper; let stand until set, about 45 minutes. Store in an airtight container at room temperature.

Nutrition Info:

- Info33 cal., 1g fat (1g sat. fat), 0 chol., 9mg sod., 6g carb. (5g sugars, 0 fiber), 1g pro.

Turkish Stuffed Apricots With Rose Water And Pistachios

Servings: 6
Cooking Time: 30 Minutes

Ingredients:

- ½ cup 2 percent Greek yogurt
- ¼ cup sugar
- ½ teaspoon rose water
- ½ teaspoon grated lemon zest plus 1 tablespoon juice
- Salt
- 2 cups water
- 4 green cardamom pods, cracked
- 2 bay leaves
- 24 whole dried apricots
- ¼ cup shelled pistachios, toasted and chopped fine

Directions:

1. Combine yogurt, 1 teaspoon sugar, rose water, lemon zest, and pinch salt in small bowl. Refrigerate filling until ready to use.
2. Bring water, cardamom pods, bay leaves, lemon juice, and remaining sugar to simmer in small saucepan over medium-low heat and cook, stirring occasionally, until sugar has dissolved, about 2 minutes. Stir in apricots, return to simmer, and cook, stirring occasionally, until plump and tender, 25 to 30 minutes. Using slotted spoon, transfer apricots to plate and let cool to room temperature.
3. Discard cardamom pods and bay leaves. Bring syrup to boil over high heat and cook, stirring occasionally, until thickened and measures about 3 tablespoons, 4 to 6 minutes; let cool to room temperature.
4. Place pistachios in shallow dish. Place filling in small zipper-lock bag and snip off 1 corner to create ½-inch opening. Pipe filling evenly into opening of each apricot and dip exposed filling into pistachios; transfer to serving platter. Drizzle apricots with syrup and serve.

Nutrition Info:

- Info150 cal., 3g fat (0g sag. fat), 0mg chol, 40mg sod., 28g carb (25g sugars, 3g fiber), 3g pro.

Mini Chocolate Cupcakes With Creamy Chocolate Frosting

Servings: 12
Cooking Time: 20 Minutes

Ingredients:

- CAKE
- 1½ ounces bittersweet chocolate, chopped
- 3 tablespoons Dutch-processed cocoa powder
- ⅓ cup hot brewed coffee
- 6 tablespoons (2 ounces) bread flour
- ¼ cup (3½ ounces) granulated sugar
- ¼ teaspoon salt
- ¼ teaspoon baking soda
- ¼ teaspoon baking powder
- 3 tablespoons canola oil
- 1 large egg
- 1 teaspoon distilled white vinegar
- ½ teaspoon vanilla extract
- CHOCOLATE FROSTING
- 2 ounces bittersweet chocolate, chopped
- 6 tablespoons unsalted butter, softened
- ½ cup (2 ounces) confectioners' sugar
- ¼ cup (¾ ounce) Dutch-processed cocoa powder
- Pinch salt
- 1 teaspoon vanilla extract

Directions:

1. FOR THE CAKE Adjust oven rack to middle position and heat oven to 350 degrees. Line 12 cups of mini muffin tin with paper or foil liners.
2. Place chocolate and cocoa in medium bowl, add hot coffee, and whisk until melted and smooth. Refrigerate mixture until completely cool, about 20 minutes. In separate bowl, whisk flour, granulated sugar, salt, baking soda, and baking powder together.
3. Whisk oil, egg, vinegar, and vanilla into cooled chocolate mixture until smooth. Add flour mixture and whisk until smooth.
4. Portion batter evenly into prepared muffin tin, filling cups to rim. Bake cupcakes until toothpick inserted in center comes out with few crumbs attached, 14 to 16 minutes, rotating muffin tin halfway through baking.
5. Let cupcakes cool in muffin tin on wire rack for 10 minutes. Remove cupcakes from muffin tin and let cool completely on rack, about 1 hour. (Unfrosted cupcakes can be stored at room temperature for up to 2 days.)
6. FOR THE FROSTING Microwave chocolate in bowl at 50 percent power, stirring occasionally, until melted and smooth, 2 to 4 minutes. Let cool slightly. Process butter, confectioners' sugar, cocoa, and salt in food processor until smooth, about 20 seconds, scraping down sides of bowl as needed. Add vanilla and process until just combined, 5 to 10 seconds. Add melted chocolate and pulse until smooth and creamy, about 10 pulses, scraping down sides of bowl as needed. (Frosting can be kept at room temperature for up to 3 hours before using or refrigerated for up to 3 days. If refrigerated, let sit at room temperature for 1 hour before using.)
7. Spread frosting evenly over cupcakes and serve.

Nutrition Info:

- Info210 cal., 13g fat (6g sag. fat), 30mg chol, 100mg sod., 22g carb (13g sugars, 2g fiber), 2g pro.

Dark Chocolate–avocado Pudding

Servings: 8
Cooking Time: 2 Hours

Ingredients:

- 1 cup water
- ¼ cup (1¾ ounces) sugar
- ¼ cup (¾ ounce) unsweetened cocoa powder
- 1 tablespoon vanilla extract
- 1 teaspoon instant espresso powder (optional)
- ¼ teaspoon salt
- 2 large ripe avocados (8 ounces each), halved and pitted
- 3½ ounces 70 percent dark chocolate, chopped

Directions:

1. Combine water, sugar, cocoa, vanilla, espresso powder (if using), and salt in small saucepan. Bring to simmer over medium heat and cook, stirring occasionally, until sugar and cocoa dissolve, about 2 minutes. Remove saucepan from heat and cover to keep warm.
2. Scoop flesh of avocados into food processor bowl and process until smooth, about 2 minutes, scraping down sides of bowl as needed. With processor running, slowly add warm cocoa mixture in steady stream until completely incorporated and mixture is smooth and glossy, about 2 minutes.
3. Microwave chocolate in bowl at 50 percent power, stirring occasionally, until melted, 2 to 4 minutes. Add to avocado mixture and process until well incorporated, about 1 minute. Transfer pudding to bowl, cover, and refrigerate until chilled and set, at least 2 hours or up to 24 hours. Serve.

Nutrition Info:

- Info170 cal., 12g fat (4g sag. fat), 0mg chol, 75mg sod., 17g carb (10g sugars, 5g fiber), 2g pro.

Cream Cheese Swirl Brownies

Servings:1
Cooking Time: 25 Minutes
Ingredients:
- 3 large eggs, divided
- 6 tablespoons reduced-fat butter, softened
- 1 cup sugar, divided
- 3 teaspoons vanilla extract
- 1/2 cup all-purpose flour
- 1/4 cup baking cocoa
- 1 package (8 ounces) reduced-fat cream cheese

Directions:
1. Preheat oven to 350°. Separate two eggs, putting each white in a separate bowl (discard yolks or save for another use); set aside. In a small bowl, beat butter and 3/4 cup sugar until crumbly. Beat in the whole egg, one egg white and vanilla until well combined. Combine flour and cocoa; gradually add to egg mixture until blended. Pour into a 9-in. square baking pan coated with cooking spray; set aside.
2. In a small bowl, beat cream cheese and remaining sugar until smooth. Beat in second egg white. Drop by rounded tablespoonfuls over the batter; cut through batter with a knife to swirl.
3. Bake 25-30 minutes or until set and edges pull away from sides of pan. Cool on a wire rack.

Nutrition Info:
- Info172 cal., 8g fat (5g sat. fat), 36mg chol., 145mg sod., 23g carb. (18g sugars, 0 fiber), 4g pro.

Grilled Angel Food Cake With Strawberries

Servings:8
Cooking Time: 15 Minutes
Ingredients:
- 2 cups sliced fresh strawberries
- 2 teaspoons sugar
- 3 tablespoons butter, melted
- 2 tablespoons balsamic vinegar
- 8 slices angel food cake (about 1 ounce each)
- Reduced-fat vanilla ice cream and blueberries in syrup, optional

Directions:
1. In a bowl, toss strawberries with sugar. In another bowl, mix butter and vinegar; brush over cut sides of cake.
2. On a greased rack, grill cake, uncovered, over medium heat about 1-2 minutes on each side or until golden brown. Serve cake with the strawberries and, if desired, the ice cream and syrup.

Nutrition Info:
- Info132 cal., 5g fat (3g sat. fat), 11mg chol., 247mg sod., 22g carb. (4g sugars, 1g fiber), 2g pro.

No-fuss Banana Ice Cream

Servings:1
Cooking Time: 15 Minutes
Ingredients:
- 6 very ripe bananas
- ½ cup heavy cream
- 1 tablespoon vanilla extract
- 1 teaspoon lemon juice
- ¼ teaspoon salt
- ¼ teaspoon ground cinnamon

Directions:
1. Peel bananas, place in large zipper-lock bag, and press out excess air. Freeze bananas until solid, at least 8 hours.
2. Let bananas sit at room temperature to soften slightly, about 15 minutes. Slice into ½-inch-thick rounds and place in food processor. Add cream, vanilla, lemon juice, salt, and cinnamon and process until smooth, about 5 minutes, scraping down sides of bowl as needed.
3. Transfer mixture to airtight container and freeze until firm, at least 2 hours or up to 5 days. Serve.

Nutrition Info:
- Info160 cal., 6g fat (3g sag. fat), 15mg chol, 75mg sod., 28g carb (18g sugars, 3g fiber), 1g pro.

Citrus Gingerbread Cookies

Servings: 6
Cooking Time: 10 Minutes

Ingredients:

- 3/4 cup sugar
- 1/2 cup honey
- 1/2 cup molasses
- 1/2 cup unsalted butter, cubed
- 1 large egg
- 3 1/2 cups all-purpose flour
- 1/4 cup ground almonds
- 2 teaspoons baking powder
- 2 teaspoons grated lemon peel
- 2 teaspoons grated orange peel
- 1 teaspoon each ground cardamom, ginger, nutmeg, cinnamon and cloves
- GLAZE
- 1/2 cup honey
- 2 tablespoons water

Directions:

1. In a large saucepan, combine sugar, honey and molasses. Bring to a boil; remove from heat. Let stand about 20 minutes. Stir in butter; let stand 20 minutes longer.
2. Beat in egg. In another bowl, whisk flour, almonds, baking powder, lemon peel, orange peel and spices; gradually beat into sugar mixture. Refrigerate, covered, 8 hours or overnight.
3. Preheat oven to 375°. On a lightly floured surface, divide dough into three portions. Roll each portion to 1/4-in. thickness. Cut with a floured 2-in. tree-shaped cookie cutter. Place 2 in. apart on baking sheets coated with cooking spray.
4. Bake 7-8 minutes or until lightly browned. Cool on pans 1 minute. Remove cookies to wire racks to cool completely. In a small bowl, mix glaze ingredients; brush over cookies. Let stand until set.

Nutrition Info:

- Info66 cal., 2g fat (1g sat. fat), 6mg chol., 13mg sod., 12g carb. (7g sugars, 0 fiber), 1g pro.

Roasted Pears With Cider Sauce

Servings: 8
Cooking Time: 10 Minutes

Ingredients:

- 3 tablespoons unsalted butter
- 4 firm but ripe pears (7 ounces each), peeled, halved, and cored
- 1 cup apple cider
- ½ teaspoon cornstarch
- ¼ cup dried cranberries, chopped
- 1 cinnamon stick
- 2 star anise pods
- 1 (2-inch) piece ginger, peeled and lightly crushed
- ⅛ teaspoon salt
- 2 tablespoons chopped toasted and skinned hazelnuts

Directions:

1. Adjust oven rack to middle position and heat oven to 450 degrees. Melt 2 tablespoons butter in 12-inch ovensafe skillet over medium-high heat. Place pear halves cut side down in skillet and cook, without moving them, until just beginning to brown, about 3 minutes.
2. Transfer skillet to oven and roast pears for 15 minutes. Using tongs, carefully flip pears cut side up and continue to roast until tip of paring knife easily pierces fruit, about 10 minutes.
3. Carefully remove skillet from oven (skillet handle will be hot) and transfer pears to platter. Whisk cider and cornstarch together in bowl. Return now-empty skillet to medium-high heat and add cider mixture, cranberries, cinnamon, star anise, ginger, and salt. Simmer vigorously, scraping up any browned bits with spoon, until sauce is thickened slightly and measures ¾ cup, 5 to 7 minutes.
4. Off heat, discard cinnamon, star anise, and ginger and stir in remaining 1 tablespoon butter. Spoon sauce over pears, sprinkle with hazelnuts, and serve.

Nutrition Info:

- Info130 cal., 6g fat (2g sag. fat), 10mg chol, 40mg sod., 22g carb (16g sugars, 3g fiber), 1g pro.

Saucy Spiced Pears

Servings: 4
Cooking Time: 20 Minutes
Ingredients:
- 1/2 cup orange juice
- 2 tablespoons butter
- 2 tablespoons sugar
- 2 teaspoons lemon juice
- 1 teaspoon vanilla extract
- 1 teaspoon ground ginger
- 1/4 teaspoon ground cinnamon
- 1/8 teaspoon salt
- 1/8 teaspoon ground allspice
- 1/8 teaspoon cayenne pepper, optional
- 3 large Bosc pears (about 1 3/4 pounds), cored, peeled and sliced
- Thinly sliced fresh mint leaves, optional

Directions:
1. In a large skillet, combine the first nine ingredients and, if desired, cayenne. Cook over medium-high heat 1-2 minutes or until butter is melted, stirring occasionally.
2. Add pears; bring to a boil. Reduce heat to medium; cook, uncovered, 3-4 minutes or until sauce is slightly thickened and pears are crisp-tender, stirring occasionally. Cool slightly. If desired, top with mint.

Nutrition Info:
- Info192 cal., 6g fat (4g sat. fat), 15mg chol., 130mg sod., 36g carb. (26g sugars, 5g fiber), 1g pro.

Individual Summer Berry Gratins

Servings: 6
Cooking Time: 10 Minutes
Ingredients:
- ¼ cup honey
- 2 tablespoons water
- 2 large egg yolks
- ½ teaspoon grated lemon zest plus 2 tablespoons juice
- Salt
- 5 ounces (1 cup) raspberries
- 5 ounces (1 cup) blackberries
- 5 ounces (1 cup) blueberries
- 1 tablespoon minced fresh tarragon
- 3 tablespoons heavy cream

Directions:
1. Adjust oven rack to upper-middle position and heat oven to 400 degrees. Line rimmed baking sheet with aluminum foil. Combine 3 tablespoons honey, water, egg yolks, lemon zest and juice, and ⅛ teaspoon salt together in medium bowl and set over saucepan filled with 1 inch of barely simmering water. Cook, whisking gently but constantly, until mixture is slightly thickened, creamy, and glossy, 5 to 10 minutes (mixture will form loose mounds when dripped from whisk).
2. Remove bowl from saucepan and whisk constantly for 30 seconds to cool slightly. Transfer bowl to refrigerator and chill until mixture is completely cool, about 10 minutes.
3. Meanwhile, gently combine raspberries, blackberries, blueberries, tarragon, and ⅛ teaspoon salt in bowl. Microwave remaining 1 tablespoon honey until loose, about 20 seconds. Drizzle warm honey over berry mixture and toss gently to coat evenly. Divide berry mixture evenly among six shallow 6-ounce gratin dishes set on prepared sheet. Bake berries until warm and just beginning to release their juices, about 8 minutes.
4. Transfer sheet to wire rack and heat broiler. Whisk heavy cream in medium bowl until it holds soft peaks, 30 to 90 seconds. Using rubber spatula, gently fold whipped cream into cooled egg mixture, then spoon mixture evenly over berries. Broil until topping is golden brown, 1 to 2 minutes, rotating sheet halfway through broiling. Serve immediately.

Nutrition Info:
- Info120 cal., 4g fat (2g sag. fat), 70mg chol, 105mg sod., 21g carb (15g sugars, 3g fiber), 2g pro.

Fig Bars

Servings: 16
Cooking Time: 45 Minutes

Ingredients:
- 1 cup (5 ounces) all-purpose flour
- 2 teaspoons ground allspice
- ½ teaspoon salt
- ¼ teaspoon baking powder
- 8 tablespoons unsalted butter, cut into ½-inch pieces and chilled
- ½ cup plus 3 tablespoons no-sugar-added apple juice
- 1 cup dried Turkish or Calimyrna figs, stemmed and quartered
- ¼ cup sliced almonds, toasted
- ¼ cup shelled pistachios, toasted and chopped

Directions:

1. Adjust oven rack to middle position and heat oven to 375 degrees. Make foil sling for 8-inch square baking pan by folding 2 long sheets of aluminum foil so each is 8 inches wide. Lay sheets of foil in pan perpendicular to each other, with extra foil hanging over edges of pan. Push foil into corners and up sides of pan, smoothing foil flush to pan. Grease foil.

2. Pulse flour, allspice, salt, and baking powder in food processor until combined, about 3 pulses. Scatter chilled butter over top and pulse until mixture resembles wet sand, about 10 pulses. Add 3 tablespoons apple juice and pulse until dough comes together, about 8 pulses.

3. Transfer mixture to prepared pan and press into even layer with bottom of dry measuring cup. Bake crust until golden brown, 35 to 40 minutes, rotating pan halfway through baking. Let crust cool completely in pan, about 45 minutes.

4. Microwave figs and remaining ½ cup apple juice in covered bowl until slightly softened, about 2 minutes. Puree fig mixture in now-empty food processor until smooth, about 15 seconds. Spread fig mixture evenly over cooled crust, then sprinkle with almonds and pistachios, pressing to adhere. Using foil overhang, lift bars from pan and transfer to cutting board. Cut into 16 squares and serve.

Nutrition Info:
- Info130 cal., 7g fat (3g sag. fat), 15mg chol, 80mg sod., 15g carb (6g sugars, 2g fiber), 2g pro.

Slow Cooker Favorites Recipes

Hearty Turkey Soup With Swiss Chard

Servings: 6
Cooking Time: 30 Minutes
Ingredients:
- 1½ pounds leeks, white and light green parts only, halved lengthwise, sliced ¼ inch thick, and washed thoroughly
- 8 ounces Swiss chard, stems chopped and leaves cut into 1-inch pieces
- 4 teaspoons extra-virgin olive oil
- 1 teaspoon no-salt-added tomato paste
- 1 teaspoon minced fresh thyme or ¼ teaspoon dried
- Salt and pepper
- 8 cups unsalted chicken broth
- 2 carrots, peeled and cut into ½-inch pieces
- 2 bay leaves
- 2 pounds bone-in turkey thighs, skin removed, trimmed of all visible fat
- ¼ cup 100 percent whole-wheat orzo

Directions:
1. Microwave leeks, chard stems, 1 tablespoon oil, tomato paste, thyme, and ½ teaspoon salt in bowl, stirring occasionally, until vegetables are softened, about 5 minutes; transfer to slow cooker. Stir in broth, carrots, and bay leaves. Nestle turkey thighs into slow cooker. Cover and cook until turkey is tender, 6 to 7 hours on low.
2. Meanwhile, bring 2 quarts water to boil in large saucepan. Add orzo and ½ teaspoon salt and cook, stirring often, until al dente. Drain orzo, rinse with cold water, then toss with remaining 1 teaspoon oil in bowl; set aside.
3. Transfer turkey to cutting board, let cool slightly, then shred into bite-size pieces using 2 forks; discard bones. Discard bay leaves.
4. Stir chard leaves into soup, cover, and cook on high until tender, 20 to 30 minutes. Stir in orzo and turkey and let sit until heated through, about 5 minutes. Season with pepper to taste. Serve.

Nutrition Info:
- Info210 cal., 6g fat (1g sag. fat), 60mg chol, 600mg sod., 17g carb (5g sugars, 4g fiber), 24g pro.

Braised Fennel With Orange-tarragon Dressing

Servings: 4
Cooking Time: 6 Hours
Ingredients:
- 2 garlic cloves, peeled and smashed
- 2 sprigs fresh thyme
- 1 teaspoon juniper berries
- 2 fennel bulbs, stalks discarded, bulbs halved, each half cut into 4 wedges
- 2 tablespoons extra-virgin olive oil
- 2 teaspoons grated orange zest plus 1 tablespoon juice
- 1 teaspoon minced fresh tarragon
- Salt and pepper

Directions:
1. Combine 1 cup water, garlic, thyme sprigs, and juniper berries in oval slow cooker. Place fennel wedges cut side down in cooker (wedges may overlap). Cover and cook until fennel is tender, 8 to 9 hours on low or 5 to 6 hours on high.
2. Whisk oil, orange zest and juice, tarragon, ¼ teaspoon salt, and ¼ teaspoon pepper together in bowl. Using slotted spoon, transfer fennel to serving dish, brushing away any garlic cloves, thyme sprigs, or juniper berries that stick to fennel. Drizzle fennel with dressing. Serve.

Nutrition Info:
- Info100 cal., 7g fat (1g sag. fat), 0mg chol, 210mg sod., 9g carb (5g sugars, 4g fiber), 2g pro.

Catalan Beef Stew

Servings: 6
Cooking Time: 10 Minutes
Ingredients:

- 2 pounds boneless beef chuck-eye roast, trimmed of all visible fat, and cut into 1½-inch pieces
- Salt and pepper
- 4 teaspoons canola oil
- 1 pound cremini mushrooms, trimmed and quartered
- 2 onions, chopped fine
- 3 tablespoons all-purpose flour
- ¼ cup no-salt-added tomato paste
- 3 garlic cloves, minced
- 1 teaspoon smoked paprika
- ¾ teaspoon ground cinnamon
- 2 cups low-sodium beef broth
- ½ cup dry white wine
- 2 (14.5-ounce) cans no-salt-added diced tomatoes, drained
- ¼ cup slivered almonds, toasted and chopped fine
- 2 tablespoons minced fresh parsley
- 1 tablespoon sherry vinegar

Directions:
1. Pat beef dry with paper towels and sprinkle with ½ teaspoon salt and ¼ teaspoon pepper. Heat 1 teaspoon oil in 12-inch skillet over medium-high heat until just smoking. Brown half of beef on all sides, about 8 minutes; transfer to slow cooker along with remaining uncooked beef.
2. Add mushrooms, onions, and remaining 1 tablespoon oil to fat left in skillet and cook over medium heat until softened and lightly browned, about 10 minutes. Stir in flour, tomato paste, garlic, paprika, and cinnamon and cook until fragrant, about 1 minute. Slowly whisk in broth and wine, scraping up any browned bits and smoothing out any lumps; transfer to slow cooker.
3. Stir tomatoes into slow cooker, cover, and cook until beef is tender, 9 to 10 hours on low or 6 to 7 hours on high. Stir in almonds, parsley, and vinegar. Season with pepper to taste. Serve.

Nutrition Info:
- Info350 cal., 13g fat (3g sag. fat), 100mg chol, 460mg sod., 16g carb (6g sugars, 3g fiber), 38g pro.

Thai-style Pork

Servings: 6
Cooking Time: 6 1/4 Hours
Ingredients:

- 1/4 cup teriyaki sauce
- 2 tablespoons rice vinegar
- 1 teaspoon crushed red pepper flakes
- 1 teaspoon minced garlic
- 2 pounds boneless pork loin chops
- 1 tablespoon cornstarch
- 1/4 cup cold water
- 1/4 cup creamy peanut butter
- Hot cooked rice
- 1/2 cup chopped green onions
- 1/2 cup dry roasted peanuts
- Lime juice, optional

Directions:
1. Mix first four ingredients. Place pork chops in a 3-qt. slow cooker; top with sauce. Cook, covered, on low until meat is tender, 6-8 hours.
2. Remove pork and cut into bite-size pieces; keep warm. Transfer cooking juices to a saucepan; bring to a boil. cornstarch and water until smooth; gradually stir into juices. Bring to a boil; cook and stir until thickened, 1-2 minutes. Stir in peanut butter. Add pork.
3. Serve with rice. Sprinkle with green onions and peanuts. If desired, drizzle with lime juice.

Nutrition Info:
- Info2/3 cup: 357 cal., 20g fat (5g sat. fat), 73mg chol., 598mg sod., 9g carb. (3g sugars, 2g fiber), 35g pro.

Chicken Thighs With Black-eyed Pea Ragout

Servings: 6
Cooking Time: 7 minutes

Ingredients:

- 1 pound kale, stemmed and chopped coarse
- 1 onion, chopped fine
- 4 garlic cloves, minced
- 1 tablespoon extra-virgin olive oil
- 1 teaspoon dry mustard
- 2 teaspoons minced fresh thyme or ½ teaspoon dried
- 2 (15-ounce) cans no-salt-added black-eyed peas, rinsed
- ½ cup unsalted chicken broth
- Salt and pepper
- 6 (5-ounce) bone-in chicken thighs, skin removed, trimmed of all visible fat
- 2 teaspoons hot sauce, plus extra for serving
- Lemon wedges

Directions:

1. Lightly coat oval slow cooker with vegetable oil spray. Microwave kale, onion, garlic, oil, mustard, and thyme in covered bowl, stirring occasionally, until vegetables are softened, 5 to 7 minutes; transfer to prepared slow cooker.
2. Process one-third of peas, broth, and ¼ teaspoon salt in food processor until smooth, about 30 seconds; transfer to slow cooker. Stir in remaining peas. Sprinkle chicken with ¼ teaspoon salt and ¼ teaspoon pepper and nestle into slow cooker. Cover and cook until chicken is tender, 4 to 5 hours on low.
3. Transfer chicken to serving platter. Stir hot sauce into ragout and season with pepper to taste. Serve chicken with ragout and lemon wedges, passing extra hot sauce separately.

Nutrition Info:

- Info 240 cal., 8g fat (1g sag. fat), 80mg chol, 380mg sod., 20g carb (4g sugars, 6g fiber), 24g pro.

Slow Cooker Split Pea Soup

Servings: 8
Cooking Time: 8 Hours

Ingredients:

- 1 package (16 ounces) dried green split peas, rinsed
- 2 cups cubed fully cooked ham
- 1 large onion, chopped
- 1 cup julienned or chopped carrots
- 3 garlic cloves, minced
- 1/2 teaspoon dried rosemary, crushed
- 1/2 teaspoon dried thyme
- 1 carton (32 ounces) reduced-sodium chicken broth
- 2 cups water

Directions:

1. In a 4- or 5-qt. slow cooker, combine all ingredients. Cover and cook on low for 8-10 hours or until peas are tender.

Nutrition Info:

- Info 260 cal., 2g fat (1g sat. fat), 21mg chol., 728mg sod., 39g carb. (7g sugars, 15g fiber), 23g pro.

Slow Cooker Mushroom Chicken & Peas

Servings: 4
Cooking Time: 3 Hours 10 Minutes

Ingredients:
- 4 boneless skinless chicken breast halves (6 ounces each)
- 1 envelope onion mushroom soup mix
- 1 cup water
- 1/2 pound sliced baby portobello mushrooms
- 1 medium onion, chopped
- 4 garlic cloves, minced
- 2 cups frozen peas, thawed

Directions:
1. Place chicken in a 3-qt. slow cooker. Sprinkle with soup mix, pressing to help seasonings adhere to chicken. Add water, mushrooms, onion and garlic.
2. Cook, covered, on low 3-4 hours or until chicken is tender (a thermometer inserted in chicken should read at least 165°). Stir in peas; cook, covered, 10 minutes longer or until heated through.

Nutrition Info:
- Info292 cal., 5g fat (1g sat. fat), 94mg chol., 566mg sod., 20g carb. (7g sugars, 5g fiber), 41g pro.

Pork Loin With Fennel, Oranges, And Olives

Servings: 8
Cooking Time: 2 Hours

Ingredients:
- 1 (2-pound) boneless center-cut pork loin roast, fat trimmed to ⅛ inch
- 1 teaspoon herbes de Provence
- Salt and pepper
- 1 tablespoon extra-virgin olive oil
- 3 fennel bulbs, stalks discarded, bulbs halved, cored, and sliced thin
- ½ cup dry white wine
- 2 garlic cloves, minced
- 4 oranges, plus 1 tablespoon grated orange zest
- ½ cup pitted kalamata olives, chopped
- 2 tablespoons minced fresh tarragon

Directions:
1. Pat roast dry with paper towels and sprinkle with herbes de Provence, ½ teaspoon salt, and ¼ teaspoon pepper. Heat oil in 12-inch skillet over medium-high heat until just smoking. Brown roast on all sides, 7 to 10 minutes; transfer to plate.
2. Add fennel and wine to now-empty skillet, cover, and cook, stirring occasionally, until fennel begins to soften, about 5 minutes. Uncover and continue to cook until fennel is dry and lightly browned, about 5 minutes. Stir in garlic and cook until fragrant, about 30 seconds; transfer to oval slow cooker. Nestle roast fat side up into slow cooker. Cover and cook until pork registers 140 degrees, 1 to 2 hours on low.
3. Transfer roast to carving board, tent with aluminum foil, and let rest for 15 minutes. Meanwhile, cut away peel and pith from oranges. Quarter oranges, then slice crosswise into ½-inch-thick pieces. Stir orange segments, orange zest, olives, and ¼ teaspoon salt into fennel mixture and let sit until heated through, about 5 minutes. Stir in tarragon and season with pepper to taste. Slice pork ½ inch thick and serve with fennel-orange mixture.

Nutrition Info:
- Info240 cal., 7g fat (1g sag. fat), 70mg chol, 350mg sod., 15g carb (10g sugars, 4g fiber), 27g pro.

Mediterranean Pot Roast Dinner

Servings: 8
Cooking Time: 8 Hours
Ingredients:
- 2 pounds potatoes (about 6 medium), peeled and cut into 2-inch pieces
- 5 medium carrots (about 3/4 pound), cut into 1-inch pieces
- 2 tablespoons all-purpose flour
- 1 boneless beef chuck roast (3 to 4 pounds)
- 1 tablespoon olive oil
- 8 large fresh mushrooms, quartered
- 2 celery ribs, chopped
- 1 medium onion, thinly sliced
- 1/4 cup sliced Greek olives
- 1/2 cup minced fresh parsley, divided
- 1 can (14 1/2 ounces) fire-roasted diced tomatoes, undrained
- 1 tablespoon minced fresh oregano or 1 teaspoon dried oregano
- 1 tablespoon lemon juice
- 2 teaspoons minced fresh rosemary or 1/2 teaspoon dried rosemary, crushed
- 2 garlic cloves, minced
- 3/4 teaspoon salt
- 1/4 teaspoon pepper
- 1/4 teaspoon crushed red pepper flakes, optional

Directions:
1. Place potatoes and carrots in a 6-qt. slow cooker. Sprinkle the flour over all surfaces of roast. In a large skillet, heat oil over medium-high heat. Brown roast on all sides. Place over vegetables.
2. Add mushrooms, celery, onion, olives and 1/4 cup parsley to slow cooker. In a small bowl, mix the remaining ingredients; pour over top.
3. Cook, covered, on low for 8-10 hours or until meat and vegetables are tender. Remove beef. Stir remaining parsley into vegetables. Serve the beef with the vegetables.

Nutrition Info:
- Info422 cal., 18g fat (6g sat. fat), 111mg chol., 538mg sod., 28g carb. (6g sugars, 4g fiber), 37g pro.

Slow Cooker Beef Tostadas

Servings: 6
Cooking Time: 6 Hours
Ingredients:
- 1 large onion, chopped
- 1/4 cup lime juice
- 1 jalapeno pepper, seeded and minced
- 1 serrano pepper, seeded and minced
- 1 tablespoon chili powder
- 3 garlic cloves, minced
- 1/2 teaspoon ground cumin
- 1 beef top round steak (about 1 1/2 pounds)
- 1 teaspoon salt
- 1/2 teaspoon pepper
- 1/4 cup chopped fresh cilantro
- 12 corn tortillas (6 inches)
- Cooking spray
- TOPPINGS
- 1 1/2 cups shredded lettuce
- 1 medium tomato, finely chopped
- 3/4 cup shredded sharp cheddar cheese
- 3/4 cup reduced-fat sour cream, optional

Directions:
1. Place the first seven ingredients in a 3- or 4-qt. slow cooker. Cut steak in half and sprinkle with salt and pepper; add to slow cooker. Cook, covered, on low 6-8 hours or until meat is tender.
2. Remove meat; cool slightly. Shred meat with two forks. Return beef to slow cooker and stir in cilantro; heat through. Spritz both sides of tortillas with cooking spray. Place in a single layer on baking sheets; broil 1-2 minutes on each side or until crisp. Spoon the beef mixture over the tortillas; top with lettuce, tomato, cheese and, if desired, sour cream.

Nutrition Info:
- Info372 cal., 13g fat (6g sat. fat), 88mg chol., 602mg sod., 30g carb. (5g sugars, 5g fiber), 35g pro.

Spiced Carrots & Butternut Squash

Servings:6
Cooking Time: 4 Hours
Ingredients:
- 5 large carrots, cut into 1/2-inch pieces (about 3 cups)
- 2 cups cubed peeled butternut squash (1-inch pieces)
- 1 tablespoon balsamic vinegar
- 1 tablespoon olive oil
- 1 tablespoon honey
- 1 teaspoon ground cinnamon
- 1/2 teaspoon salt
- 1/2 teaspoon ground cumin
- 1/4 teaspoon chili powder

Directions:
1. Place carrots and squash in a 3-qt. slow cooker. In a small bowl, mix remaining ingredients; drizzle over vegetables and toss to coat. Cook, covered, on low 4-5 hours or until vegetables are tender. Gently stir before serving.

Nutrition Info:
- Info85 cal., 3g fat (0 sat. fat), 0 chol., 245mg sod., 16g carb. (8g sugars, 3g fiber), 1g pro.

No-fuss Quinoa With Lemon

Servings:6
Cooking Time:3hours
Ingredients:
- 1½ cups prewashed white quinoa, rinsed
- 1 onion, chopped fine
- 1 tablespoon extra-virgin olive oil
- 1¾ cups water
- 2 (2-inch) strips lemon zest plus 1 tablespoon juice
- Salt and pepper
- 2 tablespoons minced fresh parsley

Directions:
1. Lightly coat slow cooker with vegetable oil spray. Microwave quinoa, onion, and 1 teaspoon oil in bowl, stirring occasionally, until quinoa is lightly toasted and onion is softened, about 5 minutes; transfer to prepared slow cooker. Stir in water, lemon zest, and ½ teaspoon salt. Cover and cook until quinoa is tender and all water is absorbed, 3 to 4 hours on low or 2 to 3 hours on high.
2. Discard lemon zest. Fluff quinoa with fork, then gently fold in lemon juice, parsley, and remaining 2 teaspoons oil. Season with pepper to taste. Serve.

Nutrition Info:
- Info190 cal., 5g fat (0g sag. fat), 0mg chol, 200mg sod., 30g carb (3g sugars, 4g fiber), 6g pro.

Chicken With Warm Potato And Radish Salad

Servings: 4
Cooking Time: 3 Hours
Ingredients:
- 1¾ pounds small Yukon Gold potatoes, unpeeled, quartered
- 2 (12-ounce) bone-in split chicken breasts, skin removed, trimmed of all visible fat, and halved crosswise
- 1 tablespoon minced fresh thyme or 1 teaspoon dried
- Salt and pepper
- 3 tablespoons extra-virgin olive oil
- 3 tablespoons minced fresh parsley
- 1 shallot, minced
- 1 tablespoon Dijon mustard
- 2 teaspoons grated lemon zest plus 2 tablespoons juice
- 5 radishes, trimmed and sliced thin

Directions:
1. Microwave potatoes and ¼ cup water in covered bowl, stirring occasionally, until almost tender, about 15 minutes; transfer to oval slow cooker. Sprinkle chicken with thyme, ¼ teaspoon salt, and ⅛ teaspoon pepper and nestle into slow cooker. Cover and cook until chicken registers 160 degrees, 2 to 3 hours on low.
2. Transfer chicken to serving platter. Whisk oil, parsley, shallot, 2 tablespoons water, mustard, lemon zest and juice, and ⅛ teaspoon salt together in large bowl. Measure out and reserve ¼ cup dressing. Drain potatoes and transfer to bowl with remaining dressing. Add radishes and toss to combine. Season with pepper to taste. Serve chicken with potato salad and reserved dressing.

Nutrition Info:
- Info440 cal., 14g fat (2g sag. fat), 100mg chol, 320mg sod., 38g carb (1g sugars, 3g fiber), 36g pro.

Parsley Smashed Potatoes

Servings: 8
Cooking Time: 6 Hours
Ingredients:
- 16 small red potatoes (about 2 pounds)
- 1 celery rib, sliced
- 1 medium carrot, sliced
- 1/4 cup finely chopped onion
- 2 cups chicken broth
- 1 tablespoon minced fresh parsley
- 1 1/2 teaspoons salt, divided
- 1 teaspoon pepper, divided
- 1 garlic clove, minced
- 2 tablespoons butter, melted
- Additional minced fresh parsley

Directions:
1. Place potatoes, celery, carrot and onion in a 4-qt. slow cooker. In a small bowl, mix broth, parsley, 1 teaspoon salt, 1/2 teaspoon pepper and garlic; pour over vegetables. Cook, covered, on low 6-8 hours or until potatoes are tender.
2. Transfer potatoes from slow cooker to a 15x10x1-in. pan; discard cooking liquid and vegetables or save for other use. Using bottom of a measuring cup, flatten potatoes slightly. Transfer to a large bowl; drizzle with butter. Sprinkle with remaining salt and pepper; toss to coat. Sprinkle with additional parsley.

Nutrition Info:
- Info114 cal., 3g fat (2g sat. fat), 8mg chol., 190mg sod., 20g carb. (2g sugars, 2g fiber), 2g pro.

Potatoes, Pasta, And Whole Grains Recipes

Penne With Butternut Squash And Sage

Servings: 6
Cooking Time: 31 minutes

Ingredients:
- 3 tablespoons extra-virgin olive oil
- 1 pound butternut squash, peeled, seeded, and cut into ½-inch pieces (2½ cups)
- 1 small head radicchio (6 ounces), halved, cored, and sliced thin
- 6 scallions, sliced thin
- 3 garlic cloves, minced
- ⅛ teaspoon ground nutmeg
- Salt and pepper
- ¾ cup dry white wine
- 1½ cups unsalted chicken broth
- 2 ounces Parmesan cheese, grated (1 cup)
- 1 ounce (2 tablespoons) mascarpone cheese
- 2 tablespoons minced fresh sage
- 1 tablespoon lemon juice
- 12 ounces (3½ cups) 100 percent whole-wheat penne
- ¼ cup sliced almonds, toasted

Directions:
1. Heat 1 tablespoon oil in 12-inch nonstick skillet over medium heat until shimmering. Add squash and cook, stirring frequently, until spotty brown, 10 to 15 minutes; transfer to bowl. Add radicchio and 1 tablespoon oil to now-empty skillet and cook over medium heat, stirring occasionally, until wilted and beginning to brown, about 1 minute. Transfer to small bowl.
2. Add remaining 1 tablespoon oil, scallions, garlic, nutmeg, and ½ teaspoon salt to now-empty skillet and cook over medium heat until scallions are softened, 1 to 2 minutes. Stir in wine, scraping up any browned bits, and cook until reduced by half, about 2 minutes.
3. Stir in broth and squash and bring to simmer. Reduce heat to low and cook until squash is tender and sauce has thickened slightly, 10 to 15 minutes. Off heat, gently stir in ½ cup Parmesan, mascarpone, sage, and lemon juice.
4. Meanwhile, bring 4 quarts water to boil in large pot. Add pasta and 1 teaspoon salt and cook, stirring often, until al dente. Reserve ½ cup cooking water, then drain pasta and return it to pot. Add squash mixture and radicchio and gently toss to combine. Adjust consistency with reserved cooking water as needed. Sprinkle individual portions with almonds and remaining ½ cup Parmesan. Serve.

Nutrition Info:
- Info390 cal., 15g fat (3g sag. fat), 15mg chol, 440mg sod., 48g carb (4g sugars, 9g fiber), 14g pro.

Brown Rice With Tomatoes And Chickpeas

Servings: 8
Cooking Time: 30 Minutes

Ingredients:

- 12 ounces grape tomatoes, quartered
- 5 scallions, sliced thin
- ¼ cup minced fresh cilantro
- 4 teaspoons extra-virgin olive oil
- 1 tablespoon lime juice
- Salt and pepper
- 2 red bell peppers, stemmed, seeded, and chopped fine
- 1 onion, chopped fine
- 1 cup long-grain brown rice, rinsed
- 4 garlic cloves, minced
- Pinch saffron threads, crumbled
- Pinch cayenne pepper
- 3¼ cups unsalted chicken broth
- 1 (15-ounce) can no-salt-added chickpeas, rinsed

Directions:

1. Combine tomatoes, scallions, cilantro, 2 teaspoons oil, lime juice, ⅛ teaspoon salt, and ⅛ teaspoon pepper in bowl; set aside for serving.
2. Heat remaining 2 teaspoons oil in 12-inch skillet over medium heat until shimmering. Add bell peppers, onion, and ¼ teaspoon salt and cook until softened and lightly browned, 8 to 10 minutes. Stir in rice, garlic, saffron, and cayenne and cook until fragrant, about 30 seconds.
3. Stir in broth, scraping up any browned bits, and bring to simmer. Reduce heat to medium-low, cover, and cook, stirring occasionally, for 25 minutes.
4. Stir in chickpeas and ⅛ teaspoon salt, cover, and cook until rice is tender and broth is almost completely absorbed, 25 to 30 minutes. Season with pepper to taste. Serve, topping individual portions with tomato mixture.

Nutrition Info:

- Info180 cal., 3g fat (0g sag. fat), 0mg chol, 210mg sod., 30g carb (4g sugars, 4g fiber), 6g pro.

Tabbouleh

Servings: 4
Cooking Time: 40 Minutes

Ingredients:

- 3 tomatoes, cored and cut into ½-inch pieces
- Salt and pepper
- ½ cup medium-grind bulgur, rinsed
- ¼ cup lemon juice (2 lemons)
- 6 tablespoons extra-virgin olive oil
- ⅛ teaspoon cayenne pepper
- 1½ cups minced fresh parsley
- ½ cup minced fresh mint
- 2 scallions, sliced thin

Directions:

1. Toss tomatoes with ¼ teaspoon salt in fine-mesh strainer set over bowl and let drain, tossing occasionally, for 30 minutes; reserve 2 tablespoons drained tomato juice. Combine bulgur, 2 tablespoons lemon juice, and reserved tomato juice in bowl and let sit until grains begin to soften, 30 to 40 minutes.
2. Whisk remaining 2 tablespoons lemon juice, oil, cayenne, and ¼ teaspoon salt together in large bowl. Add tomatoes, bulgur, parsley, mint, and scallions and gently toss to combine. Cover and let sit at room temperature until flavors have melded and grains are softened, about 1 hour. Before serving, toss salad to recombine and season with pepper to taste.

Nutrition Info:

- Info280 cal., 22g fat (3g sag. fat), 0mg chol, 320mg sod., 21g carb (3g sugars, 5g fiber), 4g pro.

Lentils With Spinach And Garlic Chips

Servings:4
Cooking Time:10 Minutes
Ingredients:
- 2 tablespoons extra-virgin olive oil
- 4 garlic cloves, sliced thin
- 1 onion, chopped fine
- Salt and pepper
- 1 teaspoon ground coriander
- 1 teaspoon ground cumin
- 2½ cups water
- 1 cup green or brown lentils, picked over and rinsed
- 8 ounces curly-leaf spinach, stemmed and chopped coarse
- 1 tablespoon red wine vinegar

Directions:
1. Cook oil and garlic in large saucepan over medium-low heat, stirring often, until garlic turns crisp and golden but not brown, about 5 minutes. Using slotted spoon, transfer garlic to paper towel–lined plate; set aside for serving.
2. Add onion and ¼ teaspoon salt to fat left in saucepan and cook over medium heat until softened and lightly browned, 5 to 7 minutes. Stir in coriander and cumin and cook until fragrant, about 30 seconds.
3. Stir in water and lentils and bring to simmer. Reduce heat to low, cover, and cook, stirring occasionally, until lentils are mostly tender but still intact, 30 to 50 minutes.
4. Stir in spinach, 1 handful at a time, and cook, stirring occasionally, until spinach is wilted and lentils are completely tender, about 8 minutes. Stir in vinegar and ⅛ teaspoon salt and season with pepper to taste. Transfer to serving dish, sprinkle with toasted garlic, and serve.

Nutrition Info:
- Info250 cal., 8g fat (1g sag. fat), 0mg chol, 270mg sod., 33g carb (2g sugars, 9g fiber), 9g pro.

Easy Greek-style Chickpea Salad

Servings:6
Cooking Time:30minutes
Ingredients:
- 3 tablespoons lemon juice
- 1 tablespoon extra-virgin olive oil
- 1 tablespoon Dijon mustard
- 1 small garlic clove, minced
- Salt and pepper
- 2 (15-ounce) cans no-salt-added chickpeas, rinsed
- 1 cucumber, peeled, halved lengthwise, seeded, and cut into ½-inch pieces
- ½ small red onion, chopped fine
- ¼ cup minced fresh mint
- 1 tablespoon minced fresh parsley
- 1 ounce feta cheese, crumbled (¼ cup)
- 2 tablespoons chopped pitted kalamata olives

Directions:
1. Whisk lemon juice, oil, mustard, garlic, and ¼ teaspoon salt together in large bowl. Add chickpeas, cucumber, onion, mint, parsley, feta, and olives and gently toss to combine. Season with pepper to taste and serve.

Nutrition Info:
- Info120 cal., 4g fat (1g sag. fat), 5mg chol, 240mg sod., 15g carb (2g sugars, 4g fiber), 6g pro.

Country Stuffed Summer Squash

Servings: 4
Cooking Time: 35 Minutes

Ingredients:
- 2 large summer squash, halved lengthwise (12 ounces total; use any variety, such as yellow, scallop, or zucchini)
- 1 cup chopped red or green bell pepper
- 1/2 cup water
- 2 tablespoons no-trans-fat margarine (35% vegetable oil)
- 1 cup dry cornbread stuffing mix

Directions:
1. Preheat the oven to 350°F.
2. Scoop out and coarsely chop the squash pulp.
3. Place a medium nonstick skillet over medium-high heat until hot. Coat the skillet with nonstick cooking spray and add the squash pulp and bell pepper. Cook 4 minutes or until the pepper is tender-crisp, stirring frequently.
4. Remove the skillet from the heat and stir in the water and margarine. Add the stuffing mix and stir gently with a fork. Spoon 1/2 cup stuffing into each squash half. Press down gently so the stuffing will adhere.
5. Recoat the skillet with nonstick cooking spray, arrange the stuffed squash in the skillet, cover tightly, and bake 30 minutes or until the squash is tender when pierced with a fork.

Nutrition Info:
- Info100 cal., 3g fat (0g sag. fat), 0mg chol, 210mg sod., 16g carb (4g sugars, 2g fiber), 3g pro.

Turkey And Cheese Lasagna

Servings: 12
Cooking Time: 26 Minutes

Ingredients:
- 1 pound (2 cups) whole-milk ricotta cheese
- 12 ounces whole-milk mozzarella cheese, shredded (3 cups)
- 1 ounce Parmesan cheese, grated (½ cup)
- 1 cup chopped fresh basil
- 1 large egg, lightly beaten
- Salt and pepper
- 1½ teaspoons extra-virgin olive oil
- 1 onion, chopped fine
- 6 garlic cloves, minced
- ¼ teaspoon dried oregano
- ⅛ teaspoon red pepper flakes
- 1 pound ground turkey
- 1 (28-ounce) can no-salt-added crushed tomatoes
- 1 (28-ounce) can no-salt-added diced tomatoes
- 16 100 percent whole-wheat lasagna noodles

Directions:
1. Mix ricotta, 2 cups mozzarella, Parmesan, ½ cup basil, egg, ¼ teaspoon salt, and ½ teaspoon pepper in bowl until well combined; cover and refrigerate until needed.
2. Heat oil in Dutch oven over medium heat until shimmering. Add onion and cook until softened, about 5 minutes. Stir in garlic, oregano, and red pepper flakes and cook until fragrant, about 30 seconds.
3. Add ground turkey and cook, breaking up meat with wooden spoon, until no longer pink, about 5 minutes. Stir in tomatoes with their juices and ¼ teaspoon salt and bring to simmer. Cook, stirring occasionally, until sauce has thickened slightly, about 15 minutes. Off heat, stir in remaining ½ cup basil, cover, and set aside.
4. Adjust oven rack to middle position and heat oven to 375 degrees. Lightly coat 13 by 9-inch baking dish with vegetable oil spray. Bring 4 quarts water to boil in large pot. Add noodles and 1 teaspoon salt and cook, stirring often, until almost al dente. Drain and rinse noodles under cold water until cool. Lay pasta out over clean kitchen towels.
5. Spread 1½ cups meat sauce over bottom of baking dish. Place 4 noodles on top of sauce and spread ¼ cup ricotta mixture evenly down center of each noodle. Spoon 1½ cups more sauce evenly over ricotta. Repeat layering two more times.
6. For final layer, place remaining 4 noodles on top and spread remaining 2 cups sauce over noodles. Sprinkle with remaining 1 cup mozzarella. Spray large sheet of aluminum foil lightly with vegetable oil spray, then cover lasagna.
7. Place lasagna on foil-lined rimmed baking sheet and bake until sauce is bubbling, 40 to 45 minutes. Uncover lasagna and continue to bake until cheese is melted and beginning to brown, about 20 minutes. Let cool for 10 to 20 minutes before serving.

Nutrition Info:
- Info350 cal., 14g fat (8g sag. fat), 70mg chol, 460mg sod., 32g carb (6g sugars, 5g fiber), 27g pro.

Paprika Roasted Potatoes

Servings: 4
Cooking Time:20 Minutes
Ingredients:
- 12 ounces new potatoes, scrubbed and quartered
- 1 teaspoon extra virgin olive oil
- 1/4 teaspoon paprika
- 1/8 plus 1/4 teaspoon salt (divided use)

Directions:
1. Preheat the oven to 350°F.
2. Arrange the potatoes on a baking pan lined with foil. Drizzle the oil over the potatoes and toss to coat completely. Sprinkle the potatoes with paprika and 1/8 teaspoon salt and bake for 20 minutes, shaking the pan after 10 minutes to stir.
3. Remove the pan from the oven and sprinkle the potatoes with 1/4 teaspoon salt. Wrap the pan tightly with foil and let stand 10 minutes.

Nutrition Info:
- Info70 cal., 1g fat (0g sag. fat), 0mg chol, 220mg sod., 14g carb (1g sugars, 2g fiber), 2g pro.

Pasta Alla Norma With Olives And Capers

Servings:6
Cooking Time: 18 Minutes
Ingredients:
- 1½ pounds eggplant, cut into ½-inch pieces
- Kosher salt and pepper
- 3½ tablespoons extra-virgin olive oil
- 4 garlic cloves, minced
- 2 anchovy fillets, rinsed and minced
- ¼ teaspoon red pepper flakes
- 1 (28-ounce) can no-salt-added crushed tomatoes
- ½ cup pitted kalamata olives, chopped coarse
- 6 tablespoons minced fresh parsley
- 2 tablespoons capers, rinsed
- 12 ounces (3⅓ cups) 100 percent whole-wheat rigatoni
- 2 ounces ricotta salata, shredded (½ cup)

Directions:
1. Line large plate with double layer of coffee filters and lightly spray with vegetable oil spray. Toss eggplant with ½ teaspoon salt, then spread out over coffee filters. Microwave eggplant, uncovered, until dry to touch and slightly shriveled, about 10 minutes, tossing halfway through cooking. Let cool slightly.
2. Transfer eggplant to large bowl, drizzle with 1 tablespoon oil, and gently toss to coat. Heat 1 tablespoon oil in 12-inch nonstick skillet over medium-high heat until shimmering. Add eggplant and cook, stirring occasionally, until well browned and fully tender, about 10 minutes; transfer to clean plate.
3. Let skillet cool slightly, about 3 minutes. Add 1 tablespoon oil, garlic, anchovies, and pepper flakes to now-empty skillet and cook over medium heat, stirring often, until garlic is lightly golden and fragrant, about 1 minute. Stir in tomatoes, increase heat to medium-high, and simmer, stirring occasionally, until slightly thickened, 8 to 10 minutes. Add eggplant and cook, stirring occasionally, until eggplant is heated through and flavors meld, 3 to 5 minutes. Stir in olives, parsley, capers, and remaining ½ tablespoon oil.
4. Meanwhile, bring 4 quarts water to boil in large pot. Add pasta and 2 teaspoons salt and cook, stirring often, until al dente. Reserve ½ cup cooking water, then drain pasta and return it to pot. Add sauce and toss to combine. Season with salt and pepper to taste and adjust consistency with reserved cooking water as needed. Serve with ricotta salata.

Nutrition Info:
- Info370 cal., 13g fat (2g sag. fat), 10mg chol, 440mg sod., 50g carb (9g sugars, 12g fiber), 12g pro.

Cuban Black Beans

Servings: 8
Cooking Time: 40 Minutes
Ingredients:
- Salt and pepper
- 1 pound dried black beans (2½ cups) picked over and rinsed
- 2 slices bacon, chopped fine
- 2 onions, chopped
- 1 red bell pepper, stemmed, seeded, and chopped
- 1 teaspoon ground cumin
- 6 garlic cloves, minced
- 2 teaspoons minced fresh oregano or ¾ teaspoon dried
- ¼ teaspoon red pepper flakes
- 3½ cups water
- 2 bay leaves
- ⅛ teaspoon baking soda
- ¼ cup minced fresh cilantro
- 1 tablespoon lime juice

Directions:
1. Dissolve 1½ tablespoons salt in 2 quarts cold water in large container. Add beans and soak at room temperature for at least 8 hours or up to 1 day. Drain and rinse well.
2. Adjust oven rack to lower-middle position and heat oven to 300 degrees. Cook bacon in Dutch oven over medium heat until crisp, 5 to 7 minutes. Stir in onions, bell pepper, cumin, and ½ teaspoon salt and cook until softened, 5 to 7 minutes. Stir in garlic, oregano, and red pepper flakes and cook until fragrant, about 30 seconds. Stir in water, scraping up any browned bits. Stir in beans, bay leaves, and baking soda and bring to simmer.
3. Cover, transfer pot to oven, and bake, stirring every 30 minutes, until beans are tender, about 1½ hours. Remove lid and continue to bake until liquid has thickened, 15 to 30 minutes, stirring halfway through cooking.
4. Discard bay leaves. Let beans sit for 10 minutes. Stir in cilantro and lime juice. Season with pepper to taste and serve.

Nutrition Info:
- Info240 cal., 3g fat (1g sag. fat), 5mg chol, 240mg sod., 40g carb (8g sugars, 6g fiber), 13g pro.

Black-eyed Peas With Walnuts And Pomegranate

Servings: 4
Cooking Time: 1 hours
Ingredients:
- 2 tablespoons extra-virgin olive oil
- 2 tablespoons lemon juice
- 2 tablespoons pomegranate molasses
- ¼ teaspoon ground coriander
- ¼ teaspoon ground cumin
- ⅛ teaspoon ground fennel seed
- Salt and pepper
- 2 (15-ounce) cans no-salt-added black-eyed peas, rinsed
- ½ cup pomegranate seeds
- ½ cup minced fresh parsley
- ⅓ cup walnuts, toasted and chopped
- 4 scallions, sliced thin

Directions:
1. Whisk oil, lemon juice, pomegranate molasses, coriander, cumin, fennel seed, ¼ teaspoon salt, and ⅛ teaspoon pepper together in large bowl until smooth. Add peas, pomegranate seeds, parsley, walnuts, and scallions and toss to combine. Season with ⅛ teaspoon salt and pepper to taste.

Nutrition Info:
- Info260 cal., 14g fat (1g sag. fat), 0mg chol, 250mg sod., 29g carb (8g sugars, 7g fiber), 9g pro.

Pasta'd Mushrooms

Servings: 4
Cooking Time:10 Minutes
Ingredients:
- 2 ounces dry, uncooked, whole-wheat spaghetti noodles, broken into thirds
- 3/4 cup finely chopped onion
- 8 ounces sliced mushrooms
- 1/4 teaspoon salt, divided use
- 1/8 teaspoon black pepper
- 2 tablespoons no-trans-fat margarine (35% vegetable oil)

Directions:
1. Cook the pasta according to package directions, omitting any salt or fat.
2. Meanwhile, place a large nonstick skillet over medium-high heat until hot. Coat the skillet with nonstick cooking spray, add the onions, and cook 3 minutes or until the onions begin to brown, stirring frequently.
3. Add the mushrooms, 1/8 teaspoon salt, and the pepper. Coat the mushroom mixture with nonstick cooking spray and cook 5 minutes longer, stirring frequently. Use two utensils to stir as you would when stir-frying.
4. Remove the skillet from the heat, stir in the margarine, and cover to keep warm.
5. Drain the pasta, reserving a little water, and stir the pasta and 1/8 teaspoon salt into the mushroom mixture. If needed, add a little pasta water to moisten.

Nutrition Info:
- Info100 cal., 3g fat (0g sag. fat), 0mg chol, 190mg sod., 16g carb (3g sugars, 3g fiber), 4g pro.

Bulgur Salad With Carrots And Almonds

Servings:8
Cooking Time:1½ Hours
Ingredients:
- 1½ cups medium-grind bulgur, rinsed
- 1 cup water
- 6 tablespoons lemon juice (2 lemons)
- Salt and pepper
- ⅓ cup extra-virgin olive oil
- ½ teaspoon ground cumin
- ⅛ teaspoon cayenne pepper
- 4 carrots, peeled and shredded
- 3 scallions, sliced thin
- ½ cup sliced almonds, toasted
- ⅓ cup chopped fresh mint
- ⅓ cup chopped fresh cilantro

Directions:
1. Combine bulgur, water, ¼ cup lemon juice, and ¼ teaspoon salt in bowl. Cover and let sit at room temperature until grains are softened and liquid is fully absorbed, about 1½ hours.
2. Whisk remaining 2 tablespoons lemon juice, oil, cumin, cayenne, and ¼ teaspoon salt together in large bowl. Add bulgur, carrots, scallions, almonds, mint, and cilantro and gently toss to combine. Season with pepper to taste. Serve.

Nutrition Info:
- Info230 cal., 13g fat (1g sag. fat), 0mg chol, 180mg sod., 26g carb (2g sugars, 6g fiber), 5g pro.

Farro Salad With Asparagus, Snap Peas, And Tomatoes

Servings: 8
Cooking Time: 15 Minutes

Ingredients:
- 6 ounces asparagus, trimmed and cut into 1-inch lengths
- 6 ounces sugar snap peas, strings removed, halved crosswise
- Salt and pepper
- 1½ cups whole farro
- 3 tablespoons extra-virgin olive oil
- 2 tablespoons lemon juice
- 2 tablespoons minced shallot
- 1 teaspoon Dijon mustard
- 6 ounces cherry tomatoes, halved
- 2 ounces feta cheese, crumbled (½ cup)
- 3 tablespoons chopped fresh dill

Directions:
1. Bring 4 quarts water to boil in large pot. Add asparagus, snap peas, and 1 teaspoon salt and cook until crisp-tender, about 3 minutes. Using slotted spoon, transfer vegetables to large plate and let cool completely, about 15 minutes.
2. Return water to boil, add farro, and cook until grains are tender with slight chew, 15 to 30 minutes. Drain farro well. Transfer to parchment paper–lined rimmed baking sheet and spread into even layer. Let cool completely, about 15 minutes.
3. Whisk oil, lemon juice, shallot, mustard, and ¼ teaspoon pepper together in large bowl. Add vegetables, farro, tomatoes, ¼ cup feta, and dill and gently toss to combine. Season with pepper to taste. Transfer to serving platter and sprinkle with remaining ¼ cup feta. Serve.

Nutrition Info:
- Info210 cal., 8g fat (2g sag. fat), 5mg chol, 120mg sod., 31g carb (4g sugars, 4g fiber), 7g pro.

Soups, Stews, And Chilis Recipes

Autumn Bisque

Servings: 12
Cooking Time: 50 Minutes
Ingredients:
- 1/4 cup buttery spread
- 2 teaspoons minced fresh chives
- 2 teaspoons minced fresh parsley
- 1/2 teaspoon grated lemon peel
- BISQUE
- 2 tablespoons olive oil
- 2 large rutabagas, peeled and cubed (about 9 cups)
- 1 large celery root, peeled and cubed (about 3 cups)
- 3 medium leeks (white portion only), chopped (about 2 cups)
- 1 large carrot, cubed (about 2/3 cup)
- 3 garlic cloves, minced
- 7 cups vegetable stock
- 2 teaspoons minced fresh thyme
- 1 1/2 teaspoons minced fresh rosemary
- 1 teaspoon salt
- 1/2 teaspoon coarsely ground pepper
- 2 cups almond milk
- 2 tablespoons minced fresh chives

Directions:
1. Mix first four ingredients. Using a melon baller or 1-teaspoon measuring spoon, shape mixture into 12 balls. Freeze on a waxed paper-lined baking sheet until firm. Transfer to a freezer container; freeze up to 2 months.
2. In a 6-qt. stock pot, heat oil over medium heat; saute rutabagas, celery root, leeks and carrot 8 minutes. Add garlic; cook and stir 2 minutes. Stir in stock, herbs, salt and pepper; bring to a boil. Reduce heat; simmer the soup, covered, until vegetables are tender, 30-35 minutes.
3. Puree soup using an immersion blender. Or, cool slightly and puree soup in batches in a blender; return to pan. Stir in milk; heat through. Top each serving with chives and herbed buttery spread ball.

Nutrition Info:
- Info146 cal., 7g fat (2g sat. fat), 0 chol., 672mg sod., 20g carb. (9g sugars, 5g fiber), 3g pro.

Chickpea And Kale Soup

Servings: 8
Cooking Time: 15 Minutes
Ingredients:
- ¼ cup extra-virgin olive oil
- 2 onions, chopped
- 2 fennel bulbs, stalks discarded, bulbs halved, cored, and chopped
- 4 ounces Spanish-style chorizo sausage, cut into ¼-inch pieces
- Salt and pepper
- 6 garlic cloves, minced
- ¼ teaspoon red pepper flakes
- 8 cups unsalted chicken broth
- 2 (15-ounce) cans no-salt-added chickpeas, rinsed
- 12 ounces kale, stemmed and chopped
- 1 teaspoon sherry vinegar, plus extra for seasoning
- 1 ounce Pecorino Romano cheese, grated (½ cup)
- ¼ cup chopped fresh parsley

Directions:
1. Heat oil in Dutch oven over medium heat until shimmering. Add onions, fennel, chorizo, ¼ teaspoon salt, and 1 teaspoon pepper and cook until vegetables are softened and lightly browned, 8 to 10 minutes. Stir in garlic and pepper flakes and cook until fragrant, about 30 seconds.
2. Stir in broth, chickpeas, and kale and bring to simmer. Reduce heat to medium-low, cover, and cook until kale is tender, about 15 minutes. Stir in vinegar and season with extra vinegar and pepper to taste. Sprinkle individual portions with Pecorino and parsley before serving.

Nutrition Info:
- Info280 cal., 14g fat (3g sag. fat), 15mg chol, 500mg sod., 24g carb (6g sugars, 7g fiber), 15g pro.

Vegetarian Chili

Servings: 6
Cooking Time: 45 Minutes

Ingredients:
- 4 teaspoons canola oil
- 1 (8-ounce) package 5-grain tempeh, crumbled into ¼-inch pieces
- 1 tablespoon cumin seeds
- 2 carrots, peeled and cut into ½-inch pieces
- 1 onion, chopped fine
- 1 red bell pepper, stemmed, seeded, and cut into ½-inch pieces
- 9 garlic cloves, minced
- 2 tablespoons chili powder
- 1 teaspoon minced canned chipotle chile in adobo sauce
- Salt and pepper
- 3 cups water
- 1 (28-ounce) can no-salt-added crushed tomatoes
- 1 (15-ounce) can no-salt-added kidney beans, rinsed
- 1 teaspoon dried oregano
- 1 cup frozen corn
- 1 zucchini, halved lengthwise, seeded, and cut into ½-inch pieces
- ½ cup minced fresh cilantro
- Lime wedges

Directions:
1. Heat 1 teaspoon oil in Dutch oven over medium-high heat until shimmering. Add tempeh and cook until browned, about 5 minutes; transfer to plate and set aside.
2. Add cumin seeds to now-empty pot and cook over medium heat, stirring often, until fragrant, about 1 minute. Stir in remaining 1 tablespoon oil, carrots, onion, bell pepper, garlic, chili powder, chipotle, and ¼ teaspoon salt and cook until vegetables are softened, 8 to 10 minutes.
3. Stir in water, tomatoes, beans, and oregano, scraping up any browned bits. Bring to simmer and cook until chili is slightly thickened, about 45 minutes.
4. Stir in corn, zucchini, and tempeh and cook until zucchini is tender, 5 to 10 minutes. Stir in cilantro and season with pepper to taste. Serve with lime wedges.

Nutrition Info:
- Info240 cal., 6g fat (0g sag. fat), 0mg chol, 220mg sod., 35g carb (9g sugars, 10g fiber), 13g pro.

Very Veggie Soup

Servings: 4
Cooking Time: 15 Minutes

Ingredients:
- 4 ounces reduced-fat pork breakfast sausage
- 2 cups coarsely chopped green cabbage (about 3/4-inch pieces)
- 1 (10-ounce) package frozen mixed vegetables
- 1 (14.5-ounce) can stewed tomatoes with liquid
- 1 1/2 cups water

Directions:
1. Place a large saucepan over medium-high heat until hot. Coat pan with nonstick cooking spray and add the sausage. Cook the sausage until no longer pink, stirring constantly, breaking up large pieces while cooking. Set aside on separate plate.
2. Recoat the pan with nonstick cooking spray, add the cabbage, and cook 3 minutes, stirring frequently. Add the remaining ingredients and bring to a boil. Reduce the heat, cover tightly, and simmer 10 minutes or until vegetables are tender.
3. Remove from the heat, stir in the sausage, cover, and let stand 5 minutes to develop flavors.

Nutrition Info:
- Info150 cal., 4g fat (1g sag. fat), 15mg chol, 330mg sod., 19g carb (8g sugars, 5g fiber), 8g pro.

Hearty Ten Vegetable Stew

Servings: 8
Cooking Time: 45 Minutes

Ingredients:

- 2 tablespoons canola oil
- 1 pound white mushrooms, trimmed and sliced thin
- Salt and pepper
- 8 ounces Swiss chard, stems chopped fine, leaves cut into ½-inch pieces
- 2 onions, chopped fine
- 1 celery rib, cut into ½-inch pieces
- 1 carrot, peeled, halved lengthwise, and sliced 1 inch thick
- 1 red bell pepper, stemmed, seeded, and cut into ½-inch pieces
- 6 garlic cloves, minced
- 2 tablespoons all-purpose flour
- 1 tablespoon no-salt added tomato paste
- 2 teaspoons minced fresh thyme or ½ teaspoon dried
- ½ cup dry white wine
- 6 cups low-sodium vegetable broth
- 1 tablespoon low-sodium soy sauce
- 8 ounces red potatoes, unpeeled, cut into 1-inch pieces
- 8 ounces celery root, peeled and cut into 1-inch pieces
- 2 parsnips, peeled and cut into 1-inch pieces
- 2 bay leaves
- 1 zucchini, halved lengthwise, seeded, and cut into ½-inch pieces
- 1 tablespoon lemon juice

Directions:

1. Heat oil in Dutch oven over medium heat until shimmering. Add mushrooms and ¼ teaspoon salt, cover, and cook until mushrooms have released their liquid, about 3 minutes. Uncover, increase heat to medium-high, and continue to cook, stirring occasionally, until mushrooms are dry and well browned, 8 to 12 minutes.
2. Stir in chard stems, onions, celery, carrot, bell pepper, and ⅛ teaspoon salt and cook until vegetables are softened and well browned, 7 to 10 minutes. Stir in garlic, flour, tomato paste, and thyme and cook until fragrant, about 1 minute. Slowly whisk in wine, scraping up any browned bits and smoothing out any lumps, and cook until nearly evaporated, about 2 minutes.
3. Stir in broth, soy sauce, potatoes, celery root, parsnips, and bay leaves and bring to simmer. Reduce heat to medium-low, partially cover, and cook until stew is thickened and vegetables are tender, about 45 minutes.
4. Stir in chard leaves and zucchini, cover, and cook until tender, 5 to 10 minutes. Discard bay leaves. Stir in lemon juice and ¼ teaspoon salt and season with pepper to taste. Serve.

Nutrition Info:

- Info160 cal., 5g fat (0g sag. fat), 0mg chol, 460mg sod., 23g carb (6g sugars, 4g fiber), 4g pro.

Sweet Corn And Peppers Soup

Servings: 5
Cooking Time: 20 Minutes

Ingredients:

- 1 cup water
- 1 pound frozen pepper and onion stir-fry
- 10 ounces frozen corn kernels, thawed
- 1 1/4 cups fat-free milk
- 2 ounces reduced-fat processed cheese (such as Velveeta), cut in small cubes
- 1/8 teaspoon black pepper

Directions:

1. In a large saucepan, bring the water to boil over high heat. Add the peppers and return to a boil. Reduce the heat, cover tightly, and simmer 15 minutes or until onions are tender.
2. Add the corn and milk. Increase the heat to high, bring just to a boil, and remove from the heat.
3. Add the remaining ingredients and 1/2 teaspoon salt, if desired, cover, and let stand 5 minutes to melt the cheese and develop flavors.

Nutrition Info:

- Info120 cal., 2g fat (0g sag. fat), 5mg chol, 220mg sod., 21g carb (10g sugars, 3g fiber), 6g pro.

Smoky Tomato Pepper Soup

Servings: 4
Cooking Time: 32 Minutes
Ingredients:
- 1 (14.5-ounce) can no-salt-added stewed tomatoes
- 8 ounces frozen pepper and onion stir-fry
- 1/2–1 medium chipotle chili pepper in adobo sauce, mashed with a fork and then finely chopped (1 1/2 teaspoons to 1 tablespoon total)
- 1 cup water
- 1 (15.5-ounce) can navy beans, rinsed and drained

Directions:
1. In a large saucepan, combine the tomatoes, peppers, chipotle pepper, and water. Bring to a boil over high heat.
2. Reduce the heat, cover tightly, and simmer 25 minutes or until onions are tender, stirring occasionally.
3. Mash the larger pieces of tomato with a fork, then add the beans and 1/4 teaspoon salt, if desired and cook 5 minutes longer.

Nutrition Info:
- Info130 cal., 1g fat (0g sag. fat), 0mg chol, 190mg sod., 26g carb (7g sugars, 9g fiber), 6g pro.

Chicken Tortilla Soup With Greens

Servings: 8
Cooking Time: 7 Minutes
Ingredients:
- 8 (6-inch) corn tortillas, cut into ½-inch strips
- 2 tablespoons canola oil
- Salt
- 1½ pounds bone-in split chicken breasts, trimmed
- 12 ounces Swiss chard, stems chopped, leaves cut into 1-inch pieces
- 1 onion, chopped fine
- 1 tablespoon no-salt-added tomato paste
- 1–3 tablespoons minced canned chipotle chile in adobo sauce
- 1 (14.5-ounce) can no-salt-added diced tomatoes, drained
- 2 garlic cloves, minced
- 8 cups unsalted chicken broth
- 1 avocado, halved, pitted, and cut into ½-inch pieces
- 1 cup fresh cilantro leaves

Directions:
1. Adjust oven rack to middle position and heat oven to 425 degrees. Toss tortilla strips with 1 tablespoon oil and spread evenly onto rimmed baking sheet. Bake, stirring occasionally, until strips are deep golden brown and crisp, 8 to 12 minutes. Sprinkle tortillas with ¼ teaspoon salt and transfer to paper towel–lined plate.
2. Pat chicken dry with paper towels. Heat remaining 1 tablespoon oil in Dutch oven over medium-high heat until just smoking. Brown chicken, 3 to 5 minutes per side; transfer to plate and discard skin.
3. Add chard stems, onion, and ½ teaspoon salt to fat left in pot and cook until softened, about 5 minutes. Stir in tomato paste, chipotle plus sauce, and tomatoes and cook until mixture is dry and slightly darkened, 5 to 7 minutes. Stir in garlic and cook until fragrant, about 30 seconds.
4. Stir in broth, scraping up any browned bits. Nestle chicken into pot along with any accumulated juices and bring to simmer. Reduce heat to medium-low, cover, and cook until chicken registers 160 degrees, 16 to 18 minutes. Transfer chicken to plate, let cool slightly, then shred into bite-size pieces using 2 forks.
5. Return soup to simmer, stir in chard leaves, and cook until mostly tender, about 5 minutes. Off heat, stir in chicken and let sit until heated through, about 5 minutes. Divide tortilla strips among individual serving bowls and ladle soup over top. Top with avocado and cilantro before serving.

Nutrition Info:
- Info270 cal., 10g fat (1g sag. fat), 60mg chol, 500mg sod., 19g carb (3g sugars, 5g fiber), 26g pro.

Butternut Squash And White Bean Soup With Sage Pesto

Servings: 8
Cooking Time: 20 Minutes

Ingredients:

- PESTO
- ⅓ cup walnuts, toasted
- 2 garlic cloves, minced
- ¾ cup fresh parsley leaves
- ⅓ cup fresh sage leaves
- ⅓ cup extra-virgin olive oil
- 1 ounce Parmesan cheese, grated (½ cup)
- SOUP
- 1 (2- to 2½-pound) butternut squash
- 4 cups unsalted chicken broth
- 3 cups water
- 1 tablespoon extra-virgin olive oil
- 1 pound leeks, white and light green parts only, halved lengthwise, sliced thin, and washed thoroughly
- 1 tablespoon no-salt-added tomato paste
- 2 garlic cloves, minced
- Salt and pepper
- 2 (15-ounce) cans no-salt-added cannellini beans
- 1 teaspoon white wine vinegar

Directions:

1. FOR THE PESTO Pulse walnuts and garlic in food processor until coarsely chopped, about 5 pulses. Add parsley and sage. With processor running, slowly add oil and process until smooth, about 1 minute, scraping down sides of bowl as needed. Transfer pesto to bowl and stir in Parmesan; set aside. (Pesto can be refrigerated for up to 3 days. To prevent browning, press plastic wrap flush to surface or top with thin layer of olive oil. Bring to room temperature before using.)
2. FOR THE SOUP Using sharp vegetable peeler or chef's knife, remove skin and fibrous threads just below skin from squash (peel until squash is completely orange with no white flesh remaining, roughly ⅛ inch deep). Cut round bulb section off squash and cut in half lengthwise. Scoop out and discard seeds; cut each half into 4 wedges.
3. Bring broth, water, and squash wedges to boil in medium saucepan over high heat. Reduce heat to medium, partially cover, and simmer vigorously until squash is very tender and starting to fall apart, about 20 minutes. Using potato masher, mash squash, still in broth, until completely broken down. Cover to keep warm; set aside.
4. Meanwhile, cut neck of squash into ⅓-inch cubes. Heat oil in Dutch oven over medium heat until shimmering. Add leeks and tomato paste and cook, stirring occasionally, until leeks are softened and tomato paste is darkened, about 5 minutes. Stir in garlic and cook until fragrant, about 30 seconds. Add squash pieces, ¼ teaspoon salt, and ¼ teaspoon pepper and cook, stirring occasionally, for 5 minutes. Add squash broth and bring to simmer. Partially cover and cook for 10 minutes.
5. Stir in beans and their liquid, partially cover, and cook, stirring occasionally, until squash is just tender, 15 to 20 minutes. Stir in vinegar. Top each individual portion with 1 tablespoon pesto before serving.

Nutrition Info:

- Info270 cal., 16g fat (2g sag. fat), 5mg chol, 240mg sod., 26g carb (5g sugars, 6g fiber), 9g pro.

Black Bean-tomato Chili

Servings: 6
Cooking Time: 35 Minutes

Ingredients:

- 2 tablespoons olive oil
- 1 large onion, chopped
- 1 medium green pepper, chopped
- 3 garlic cloves, minced
- 1 teaspoon ground cinnamon
- 1 teaspoon ground cumin
- 1 teaspoon chili powder
- 1/4 teaspoon pepper
- 3 cans (14 1/2 ounces each) diced tomatoes, undrained
- 2 cans (15 ounces each) black beans, rinsed and drained
- 1 cup orange juice or juice from 3 medium oranges

Directions:

1. In a Dutch oven, heat the oil over medium-high heat. Add onion and green pepper; cook and stir for 8-10 minutes or until tender. Add garlic and seasonings; cook 1 minute longer.
2. Stir in remaining ingredients; bring to a boil. Reduce heat; simmer, covered, 20-25 minutes to allow flavors to blend, stirring occasionally.

Nutrition Info:

- Info232 cal., 5g fat (1g sat. fat), 0 chol., 608mg sod., 39g carb. (13g sugars, 10g fiber), 9g pro.

Pumpkin Turkey Chili

Servings: 8
Cooking Time: 30 Minutes

Ingredients:

- 1 pound ground turkey
- 1 tablespoon plus 2 cups water, plus extra as needed
- Salt and pepper
- ¼ teaspoon baking soda
- 4 dried ancho chiles, stemmed, seeded, and torn into ½-inch pieces (1 cup)
- 1½ tablespoons ground cumin
- 1½ teaspoons ground coriander
- 1½ teaspoons dried oregano
- 1½ teaspoons paprika
- 1 (28-ounce) can no-salt-added whole peeled tomatoes
- 2 tablespoons extra-virgin olive oil
- 2 onions, chopped fine
- 2 red bell peppers, stemmed, seeded, and cut into ½-inch pieces
- 6 garlic cloves, minced
- 1 cup canned unsweetened pumpkin puree
- 2 (15-ounce) cans no-salt-added black beans, rinsed
- ¼ cup chopped fresh cilantro
- Lime wedges

Directions:

1. Toss turkey, 1 tablespoon water, ¼ teaspoon salt, and baking soda in bowl until thoroughly combined. Set aside for 20 minutes.
2. Toast anchos in Dutch oven over medium-high heat, stirring frequently, until fragrant, 4 to 6 minutes; transfer to food processor and let cool slightly. Add cumin, coriander, oregano, paprika, and 1 teaspoon pepper and process until finely ground, about 2 minutes; transfer to bowl. Process tomatoes and their juice in now-empty food processor until smooth, about 30 seconds.
3. Heat oil in now-empty pot over medium heat until shimmering. Add onions, bell peppers, and ¾ teaspoon salt and cook until softened, 8 to 10 minutes. Increase heat to medium-high, add turkey, and cook, breaking up meat with wooden spoon, until no longer pink, 4 to 6 minutes. Stir in spice mixture and garlic and cook until fragrant, about 30 seconds. Stir in tomatoes, pumpkin, and remaining 2 cups water and bring to simmer. Reduce heat to low, cover, and cook, stirring occasionally, for 1 hour.
4. Stir in beans, cover, and cook until slightly thickened, about 45 minutes. (If chili begins to stick to bottom of pot or looks too thick, stir in extra water as needed.) Season with pepper to taste. Sprinkle individual portions with cilantro and serve with lime wedges.

Nutrition Info:

- Info240 cal., 6g fat (1g sag. fat), 20mg chol, 460mg sod., 26g carb (6g sugars, 9g fiber), 22g pro.

Tomato-orange Soup

Servings: 6
Cooking Time: 1 Hour

Ingredients:

- 3 pounds tomatoes, halved
- 2 tablespoons canola oil, divided
- 2 medium onions, chopped
- 2 garlic cloves, minced
- 3 cups reduced-sodium chicken broth
- 1 cup orange juice
- 2 tablespoons tomato paste
- 4 teaspoons grated orange peel
- 1 tablespoon butter
- 1 tablespoon minced fresh cilantro
- 1 tablespoon honey
- 1/4 teaspoon salt

Directions:

1. Preheat oven to 450°. Place the tomatoes in a 15x10x1-in. baking pan, cut side down; brush tomato tops with 1 tablespoon oil. Roast 20-25 minutes or until skins are blistered and charred. Remove and discard skins.
2. In a 6-qt. stockpot, heat remaining oil over medium-high heat. Add onions; cook and stir until tender. Add garlic; cook 1 minute longer. Stir in broth, orange juice, tomato paste and roasted tomatoes; bring to a boil. Reduce heat; simmer, uncovered, 45 minutes.
3. Stir in orange peel, butter, cilantro, honey and salt. Remove from heat; cool slightly. Process soup in batches in a blender until smooth. Return to pot; heat through.

Nutrition Info:

- Info160 cal., 7g fat (2g sat. fat), 5mg chol., 419mg sod., 22g carb. (15g sugars, 4g fiber), 5g pro.

New England Fish Stew

Servings: 4
Cooking Time: 15 Minutes
Ingredients:
- 1 teaspoon canola oil
- 1 slice bacon, chopped fine
- 1 onion, chopped
- Salt and pepper
- 4½ teaspoons all-purpose flour
- ½ teaspoon minced fresh thyme or ⅛ teaspoon dried
- 2 (8-ounce) bottles clam juice
- ½ cup water
- ¼ cup dry white wine
- 8 ounces red potatoes, unpeeled, cut into 1-inch pieces
- 1 bay leaf
- 1½ pounds skinless cod fillets, ¾ to 1 inch thick, cut into 1½-inch pieces
- ⅓ cup half-and-half
- 2 tablespoons chopped fresh parsley

Directions:
1. Heat oil in Dutch oven over medium heat until shimmering. Add bacon and cook until rendered and crisp, 5 to 7 minutes. Stir in onion and ⅛ teaspoon salt and cook until softened, about 5 minutes. Stir in flour and thyme and cook until fragrant, about 1 minute. Slowly whisk in clam juice, water, and wine, scraping up any browned bits and smoothing out any lumps.
2. Stir in potatoes and bay leaf and bring to simmer. Cover, reduce heat to medium-low, and cook until potatoes are almost tender, about 15 minutes.
3. Nestle cod pieces into stew, cover, and cook until fish flakes apart when gently prodded with paring knife and registers 140 degrees, 8 to 10 minutes.
4. Discard bay leaf. Off heat, stir in half-and-half and parsley and season with pepper to taste. Serve.

Nutrition Info:
- Info280 cal., 7g fat (2g sag. fat), 90mg chol, 480mg sod., 15g carb (3g sugars, 2g fiber), 34g pro.

Mushroom And Wheat Berry Soup

Servings: 8
Cooking Time: 10 Minutes
Ingredients:
- 1 cup wheat berries, rinsed
- 3 tablespoons extra-virgin olive oil
- 1½ pounds cremini mushrooms, trimmed and sliced thin
- ¼ teaspoon salt
- 1 onion, chopped fine
- 6 garlic cloves, minced
- 2 teaspoons no-salt-added tomato paste
- 1 cup dry sherry
- 8 cups unsalted chicken broth
- 1 tablespoon low-sodium soy sauce
- 1 sprig fresh thyme
- 1 bay leaf
- ½ ounce dried shiitake mushrooms, finely ground using spice grinder
- 4 ounces mustard greens, stemmed and chopped
- ¼ teaspoon grated lemon zest plus 2 teaspoons juice

Directions:
1. Toast wheat berries in Dutch oven over medium heat, stirring often, until fragrant and beginning to darken, about 5 minutes; transfer to bowl.
2. Heat 2 tablespoons oil in now-empty pot over medium heat until shimmering. Add cremini mushrooms and salt, cover, and cook until mushrooms have released their liquid, about 3 minutes. Uncover, increase heat to medium-high, and continue to cook, stirring occasionally, until mushrooms are dry and begin to brown, 5 to 7 minutes; transfer to plate.
3. Heat remaining 1 tablespoon oil in now-empty pot over medium heat until shimmering. Add onion and cook until softened, about 5 minutes. Stir in garlic and tomato paste and cook until slightly darkened, about 2 minutes.
4. Stir in sherry, scraping up any browned bits, and cook until nearly evaporated, about 2 minutes. Stir in wheat berries, broth, soy sauce, thyme sprig, bay leaf, and shiitakes and bring to simmer. Reduce heat to low, cover, and cook until wheat berries are tender but still chewy, 45 minutes to 1 hour.
5. Discard thyme sprig and bay leaf. Off heat, stir in cremini mushrooms and any accumulated juices, mustard greens, and lemon zest. Cover and let sit until greens are wilted, about 5 minutes. Stir in lemon juice. Serve.

Nutrition Info:
- Info210 cal., 6g fat (1g sag. fat), 0mg chol, 280mg sod., 26g carb (4g sugars, 5g fiber), 10g pro.

28 day meal plan

Day 1
Breakfast: Popcorn With Olive Oil
Lunch: Zesty Lemony Shrimp
Dinner: Blueberry Salsa

Day 2
Breakfast: Southwest Breakfast Pockets
Lunch: Dilled Chex Toss
Dinner: Spring Chicken & Pea Salad

Day 3
Breakfast: Avocado And Bean Toast
Lunch: Raisin & Hummus Pita Wedges
Dinner: Roasted Beans And Green Onions

Day 4
Breakfast: Sausage-egg Burritos
Lunch: Garden-fresh Wraps
Dinner: Orzo With Peppers & Spinach

Day 5
Breakfast: Toasted Corn Salsa
Lunch: Minutesi Feta Pizzas
Dinner: Sautéed Spinach With Yogurt And Dukkah

Day 6
Breakfast: Sweet Onion Frittata With Ham
Lunch: Southwest-style Shepherd's Pie
Dinner: Basil Grilled Corn On The Cob

Day 7
Breakfast: Breakfast Tacos
Lunch: Turkey-thyme Stuffed Peppers
Dinner: Broiled Eggplant With Basil

Day 8
Breakfast: Crunchy French Toast
Lunch: Sausage Orecchiette Pasta
Dinner: Crunchy Pear And Cilantro Relish

Day 9
Breakfast: Raspberry Peach Puff Pancake
Lunch: Country Roast Chicken With Lemony Au Jus
Dinner: Roasted Root Vegetables With Lemon-caper Sauce

Day 10
Breakfast: Marinated Artichokes
Lunch: Avocado And Green Chili Chicken
Dinner: Sautéed Swiss Chard With Garlic

Day 11
Breakfast: Cheesy Baked Grits
Lunch: Braised Chicken Breasts With Chickpeas And Chermoula
Dinner: Balsamic Zucchini Saute

Day 12
Breakfast: Kale Chips
Lunch: Baked Chicken Chalupas
Dinner: Pesto Pasta & Potatoes

Day 13
Breakfast: Crispy Polenta Squares With Olives And Sun-dried Tomatoes
Lunch: Pan-seared Chicken Breasts With Leek And White Wine Pan Sauce
Dinner: Tomato-onion Green Beans

Day 14
Breakfast: Egg & Hash Brown Breakfast Cups
Lunch: Sausage And Farro Mushrooms
Dinner: Marinated Eggplant With Capers And Mint

Day 15
Breakfast: Avocado Endive Boats
Lunch: Quick & Easy Turkey Sloppy Joes
Dinner: Sautéed Green Beans With Garlic And Herbs

Day 16
Breakfast: Bleu Cheese'd Pears
Lunch: Bacon & Swiss Chicken Sandwiches
Dinner: Saucy Eggplant And Capers

Day 17
Breakfast: Chicken, Mango & Blue Cheese Tortillas
Lunch: Lemon Chicken With Orzo
Dinner: Chickpea Cakes With Cucumber-yogurt Sauce

Day 18
Breakfast: Fantastic Fish Tacos
Lunch: Turkey Shepherd's Pie
Dinner: Stewed Chickpeas With Eggplant And Tomatoes

Day 19
Breakfast: Sweet Potato, Poblano, And Black Bean Tacos
Lunch: Shrimp-slaw Pitas
Dinner: Mexican-style Spaghetti Squash Casserole

Day 20
Breakfast: Vegan Black Bean Burgers
Lunch: Garlic-herb Salmon Sliders
Dinner: Light Parmesan Pasta

Day 21
Breakfast: Roasted Winter Squash Salad With Za'atar And Parsley
Lunch: Poached Snapper With Sherry-tomato Vinaigrette
Dinner: Stuffed Eggplant With Bulgur

Day 22
Breakfast: Broccoli & Apple Salad
Lunch: Shrimp And Sausage Rice
Dinner: Curried Tempeh With Cauliflower And Peas

Day 23
Breakfast: Spicy Chipotle Chicken Salad With Corn
Lunch: Lemon-pepper Tilapia With Mushrooms
Dinner: Cheesy Spinach-stuffed Shells

Day 24
Breakfast: Tangy Sweet Carrot Pepper Salad
Lunch: Tomato-poached Halibut
Dinner: Eggplant Involtini

Day 25
Breakfast: Shrimp Salad With Avocado And Grapefruit
Lunch: Salmon Cakes With Lemon-herb Sauce
Dinner: Sautéed Spinach With Chickpeas And Garlicky Yogurt

Day 26
Breakfast: Michigan Cherry Salad
Lunch: Black Rice Bowls With Salmon
Dinner: Ricotta-stuffed Portobello Mushrooms

Day 27
Breakfast: Toasted Pecan And Apple Salad
Lunch: Shrimp Piccata
Dinner: "refried" Bean And Rice Casserole

Day 28
Breakfast: Warm Cabbage Salad With Chicken
Lunch: Pan-seared Sesame-crusted Tuna Steaks
Dinner: Tunisian-style Grilled Vegetables With Couscous And Eggs

INDEX

"refried" Bean And Rice Casserole 50

A
Arugula Salad With Fennel And Shaved Parmesan 57
Autumn Bisque 88
Avocado And Bean Toast 11
Avocado And Green Chili Chicken 25
Avocado Endive Boats 17

B
Bacon & Swiss Chicken Sandwiches 28
Baked Chicken Chalupas 26
Baked Pot Stickers With Dipping Sauce 21
Balsamic Zucchini Saute 41
Basil Grilled Corn On The Cob 39
Black Bean-tomato Chili 92
Black Rice Bowls With Salmon 34
Black-eyed Peas With Walnuts And Pomegranate 85
Bleu Cheese'd Pears 18
Blueberry Salsa 20
Braised Chicken Breasts With Chickpeas And Chermoula 25
Braised Fennel With Orange-tarragon Dressing 73
Braised Pork Stew 64
Breakfast Tacos 13
Broccoli & Apple Salad 52
Broiled Eggplant With Basil 39
Brown Rice With Tomatoes And Chickpeas 81
Brussels Sprout Salad With Pecorino And Pine Nuts 58
Bulgur Salad With Carrots And Almonds 86
Butternut Squash And White Bean Soup With Sage Pesto 92

C
Cabbage Roll Skillet 61
Cajun Beef & Rice 59
Catalan Beef Stew 74
Cheesy Baked Grits 15
Cheesy Spinach-stuffed Shells 47
Chicken Thighs With Black-eyed Pea Ragout 75
Chicken Tortilla Soup With Greens 91
Chicken With Warm Potato And Radish Salad 79
Chicken, Mango & Blue Cheese Tortillas 18
Chickpea And Kale Soup 88
Chickpea Cakes With Cucumber-yogurt Sauce 43
Chili Sloppy Joes 61
Chocolate-dipped Strawberry Meringue Roses 67
Citrus Gingerbread Cookies 70

Classic Wedge Salad 54
Cod In Coconut Broth With Lemon Grass And Ginger 37
Country Roast Chicken With Lemony Au Jus 24
Country Stuffed Summer Squash 83
Cream Cheese Swirl Brownies 69
Creamy Dill Sauce 36
Crispy Polenta Squares With Olives And Sun-dried Tomatoes 16
Crostini With Kalamata Tomato 19
Crunchy French Toast 13
Crunchy Pear And Cilantro Relish 40
Cuban Black Beans 85
Cumin'd Beef Patties And Santa Fe Sour Cream 62
Curried Tempeh With Cauliflower And Peas 47

D
Dark Chocolate–avocado Pudding 68
Dilled Chex Toss 18

E
Easy Greek-style Chickpea Salad 82
Egg & Hash Brown Breakfast Cups 16
Eggplant Involtini 49

F
Fantastic Fish Tacos 37
Farro Salad With Asparagus, Snap Peas, And Tomatoes 87
Fig Bars 72
Frozen Chocolate Monkey Treats 66

G
Garden Bounty Potato Salad 54
Garden-fresh Wraps 20
Garlic-herb Salmon Sliders 31
Grilled Angel Food Cake With Strawberries 69

H
Hearty Ten Vegetable Stew 90
Hearty Turkey Soup With Swiss Chard 73

I
Individual Summer Berry Gratins 71

K
Kale Chips 15

L

Lemon Chicken With Orzo 29
Lemon Cupcakes With Strawberry Frosting 66
Lemon-pepper Tilapia With Mushrooms 33
Lentils With Spinach And Garlic Chips 82
Light Parmesan Pasta 45
Lime'd Blueberries 22

M

Marinated Artichokes 14
Marinated Eggplant With Capers And Mint 42
Meatballs In Cherry Sauce 22
Mediterranean Pot Roast Dinner 77
Mexican-style Spaghetti Squash Casserole 44
Michigan Cherry Salad 55
Mini Chocolate Cupcakes With Creamy Chocolate Frosting 68
Minutesi Feta Pizzas 21
Mushroom And Wheat Berry Soup 94

N

New England Fish Stew 94
No-fuss Banana Ice Cream 69
No-fuss Quinoa With Lemon 78

O

One-pot Beef & Pepper Stew 62
Orzo With Peppers & Spinach 38

P

Pan-seared Chicken Breasts With Leek And White Wine Pan Sauce 26
Pan-seared Sesame-crusted Tuna Steaks 35
Paprika Roasted Potatoes 84
Parsley Smashed Potatoes 79
Pasta Alla Norma With Olives And Capers 84
Pasta'd Mushrooms 86
Penne With Butternut Squash And Sage 80
Peppered Beef Tenderloin 59
Pesto Pasta & Potatoes 41
Poached Snapper With Sherry-tomato Vinaigrette 32
Popcorn With Olive Oil 10
Pork Loin With Fennel, Oranges, And Olives 76
Pumpkin Turkey Chili 93

Q

Quick & Easy Turkey Sloppy Joes 27
Quick Hawaiian Pizza 64

R

Raisin & Hummus Pita Wedges 19
Raspberry Peach Puff Pancake 14
Ricotta-stuffed Portobello Mushrooms 50
Roasted Beans And Green Onions 38
Roasted Pears With Cider Sauce 70
Roasted Red Pepper Tapenade 19
Roasted Root Vegetables With Lemon-caper Sauce 40
Roasted Winter Squash Salad With Za'atar And Parsley 52

S

Salmon Cakes With Lemon-herb Sauce 34
Saucy Eggplant And Capers 42
Saucy Spiced Pears 71
Sausage And Farro Mushrooms 27
Sausage Orecchiette Pasta 24
Sausage-egg Burritos 11
Sautéed Green Beans With Garlic And Herbs 42
Sautéed Spinach With Chickpeas And Garlicky Yogurt 49
Sautéed Spinach With Yogurt And Dukkah 39
Sautéed Swiss Chard With Garlic 40
Shrimp And Sausage Rice 32
Shrimp Piccata 35
Shrimp Salad With Avocado And Grapefruit 55
Shrimp-slaw Pitas 31
Slow Cooker Beef Tostadas 77
Slow Cooker Mushroom Chicken & Peas 76
Slow Cooker Split Pea Soup 75
Smoky Sirloin 60
Smoky Tomato Pepper Soup 91
Southwest Breakfast Pockets 10
Southwest-style Shepherd's Pie 23
Spiced Carrots & Butternut Squash 78
Spicy Chili'd Sirloin Steak 65
Spicy Chipotle Chicken Salad With Corn 53
Spinach Steak Pinwheels 60
Spring Chicken & Pea Salad 28
Steak Tacos With Jícama Slaw 63
Stewed Chickpeas With Eggplant And Tomatoes 44
Stuffed Eggplant With Bulgur 46
Sunday Pork Roast 65
Sweet Corn And Peppers Soup 90
Sweet Jerk Pork 63
Sweet Onion Frittata With Ham 12
Sweet Potato, Poblano, And Black Bean Tacos 45

T

Tabbouleh 81
Tangy Sweet Carrot Pepper Salad 53
Thai-style Pork 74
Toasted Corn Salsa 12
Toasted Pecan And Apple Salad 56
Tomato-onion Green Beans 41
Tomato-orange Soup 93
Tomato-poached Halibut 33
Tunisian-style Grilled Vegetables With Couscous And Eggs 51
Turkey And Cheese Lasagna 83
Turkey Shepherd's Pie 30
Turkey-thyme Stuffed Peppers 23
Turkish Stuffed Apricots With Rose Water And Pistachios 67
Two-sauce Cajun Fish 36

V

Vegan Black Bean Burgers 48
Vegetarian Chili 89
Very Veggie Soup 89

W

Walnut Vinaigrette 57
Warm Cabbage Salad With Chicken 56
Warm Spinach Salad With Apple, Blue Cheese, And Pecans 58

Z

Zesty Lemony Shrimp 17

Printed in Great Britain
by Amazon